STEUBEN

SEVENTY YEARS OF
AMERICAN GLASSMAKING

STEUBEN

PAUL N. PERROT
PAUL V. GARDNER
JAMES S. PLAUT

SEVENTY YEARS OF AMERICAN GLASSMAKING

PRAEGER PUBLISHERS
NEW YORK · WASHINGTON

This edition was prepared for the exhibition "Steuben: Seventy Years of American Glassmaking," 1974–76, in cooperation with The Toledo Museum of Art.

On the front cover: *The Myth of Adonis*, 1966. Collection of the Brady Hill Company, Birmingham, Michigan.

On the back cover: Gold Aurene glass, *ca.* 1904–1920s. Collection of the Smithsonian Institution, Washington, D.C. (Wagner Collection) and private collections.

Published in the United States of America in 1974
by Praeger Publishers, Inc.
111 Fourth Avenue, New York, N.Y. 10003

Second printing, 1975

Library of Congress Cataloging in Publication Data
Main entry under title:
Steuben: 70 years of American glassmaking.
   Catalog of the exhibition held at the Toledo Museum of Art and various other museums throughout the United States beginning Nov. 1974 and lasting two years.
   1. Steuben Glass, inc.   2. Glassware,   American — Exhibitions.
I. Toledo Museum of Art.

NK5101.T62T647   748.2′9147′83   74-6730
ISBN 0-275-44320-5

Design and Layout by Gilda Kuhlman

Printed in the United States of America

List of Museums Participating in the Exhibition
"Steuben: Seventy Years of American Glassmaking," 1974–76

The Toledo Museum of Art
Toledo, Ohio

National Museum of History and Technology
Smithsonian Institution
Washington, D.C.

The Corning Museum of Glass
Corning, New York

The Art Institute of Chicago
Chicago, Illinois

The Minneapolis Institute of Art
Minneapolis, Minnesota

Amon Carter Museum of Western Art
Fort Worth, Texas

Virginia Museum of Fine Arts
Richmond, Virginia

Royal Ontario Museum
Toronto, Ontario, Canada

Museum of Fine Arts
Boston, Massachusetts

CONTENTS

PREFACE

The occasion that prompts this book is a nationwide exhibition of Steuben glass organized by the Toledo Museum of Art to celebrate seventy years of fine American glass production. For the exhibition, major examples were selected from the vast, varied, and distinguished production of this great glass house, whose name has always been associated with the very highest quality of American glassmaking.

The Steuben production falls naturally into two main periods: the years under the direction of Frederick Carder, from the founding of the original Steuben Glass Works in 1903 until 1932; and the period when the firm was under the direction of Arthur A. Houghton, Jr., from the foundation of a new Steuben Glass within Corning Glass Works, until Houghton's retirement in 1972.

The history of this celebrated glass house is, like that of so many other successful enterprises, the story of two strong personalities who gave a specific character to the glass produced under their direction. Carder's interest in complex techniques and in a wide range of colors was succeeded by Houghton's elegant restraint and his persistent search for perfection, which resulted in a purity and quality that have yet to be surpassed.

The leadership of these two men, and the glass that resulted from it, are described in the three essays that follow, and in the illustrations of the glass selected for this seventieth anniversary celebration.

This exhibition was initiated and organized by the Toledo Museum of Art, which, in addition to its own extensive permanent collections of ancient, European, and American glass, has for many years held temporary exhibitions pertaining to various aspects of glass.

We wish to express our thanks to Steuben Glass, which has lent the major portion of the glass shown, and to those private collectors and museums that have generously allowed their glass to travel to major American and Canadian museums. We are especially grateful to the Government of Canada for allowing that splendid achievement of Steuben Glass, the Great Ring of Canada, presented to that country by President Johnson in 1967, to be included in the exhibition.

Neither the exhibition nor this publication would have been possible without the inspiration and constant encouragement of Thomas S. Buechner, now president of Steuben Glass, of Francis S. Mason, Jr., his assistant, who at every turn was so helpful with the complex organization of the exhibition, and of so many others associated over the years with the Steuben production. The exhibition and this book may be said, in fact, to bring into proper focus the artistry and craftsmanship of Steuben's glassworkers, engravers, and designers over the years. The design and installation of the exhibition are by Bernard X. Wolff.

We are grateful for the editorial initiative of Brenda Gilchrist at Praeger Publishers and for the counsel of Ellyn Childs, who has guided the book from its inception with such care.

A continuing and steadfast search for quality, rather than quantity, has characterized Steuben Glass since its inception. It is a tradition now seventy years old, an uninterrupted span rarely matched in the history of glass. It should be applauded and celebrated. That is the purpose of this publication and exhibition.

Otto Wittmann, Director
The Toledo Museum of Art
Toledo, Ohio

STEUBEN

SEVENTY YEARS OF
AMERICAN GLASSMAKING

INTRODUCTION

PAUL N. PERROT

Throughout the past three-and-a-half millennia, glass, that infinitely versatile material, has been exploited and praised for the enormous range of colors and textures it can be made to display through careful formulation and handling and for its optical qualities. For some, glass is color, a juxtaposition of deep hues, emerging from the mass or appearing in shimmering nuances on the surface. For them, glass is a palette turned into a three-dimensional canvas, ever changing under the effect of light, yet primarily important for its inner color. For others, glass is almost a negation of its substance: Glass is light—not merely a magnifier, a reflector, or refractor of light but almost an originator of light. The purer the formulation, the heavier the mass, the greater the optical effect—an effect that, given the right circumstances, will originate within, giving light a tangible, three-dimensional, tactile quality. These interior effects can be magnified and altered by a careful manipulation of the surface that causes the light to reflect and refract in shimmering, sparkling patterns that do not necessarily break down the sculptural effect of a form, but give it a quality found in no other material, except rock crystal.

Not often does one firm become pre-eminent in two such opposing modes of glassmaking. That Steuben Glass has been such a firm is due to the dominant personality of its founder, Frederick Carder, and to the master orchestrator of its reorganization and revitalization, Arthur A. Houghton, Jr.

It is hard to conceive of two more distinctly different individuals. One, a consummate technician, craftsman, and artist, who rose—almost self-taught, tempered by the heat of the furnace—by hard work, personal experience, and unflagging initiative. After being taught, Carder became a teacher; from a follower, he became a leader. A man of exacting personal standards, he exemplified the independence, initiative, and tenacity of the self-directed. His successor was an intellectual, with patrician tastes, a broad view of history, a strong sense of social responsibility, and keen business acumen. He was an orchestrator of forces, often far in advance of his time, concerned with innumerable aspects of human endeavor in that stimulating, prescient manner which is the hallmark of the true connoisseur.

These two men formed Steuben Glass, and this book and exhibition display the essence of their combined achievements. The products developed by the firm during their tenure—even though neither director may have had a direct involvement in their design or manufacture—reflect their personalities and their views of the material.

It is impossible to understand the early history of Steuben Glass without taking a look at the glass produced at the end of the nineteenth century. This was an active period, in which companies on both sides of the Atlantic were vying with each other in developing new formulas, and such individual artists as Emile Gallé were assuming a role in industry. The incubus of the Industrial Revolution, the uniformity (no matter how varied in its detail) of machine production, the deadening effect of the pressing machine upon the supremacy of the head glassblower, or "gaffer," had found an antidote in Art Glass, which, in some of its manifestations, was almost as meretricious as what it was replacing—but it opened new vistas as well. At this time, too, Art Nouveau became an influence upon all the arts and crafts—that extraordinary style based on natural forms, rhythmically intertwined, emerging from and dissolving into the mass to form totalities in which design, function, color, and texture are all so interwoven that a kind of "natural" permanence seems to imbue even the simplest objects.

Frederick Carder grew up during the period when all of these tendencies were at work. He absorbed an interest in Victorian textures and techniques, and came under the spell of Art Nouveau. Then, yielding to what seemingly were attractive offers, he removed himself from the mainstream of glassmaking activity in England to come to Corning, New York, and founded a glass factory where he hoped to have the independence necessary to give fruition to his ideas.

In retrospect, we see that some of his ideas were not quite as original as he may have thought. But that in no way detracts either from Carder or from his accomplishments. Man is a product of his time, and either he expresses himself by summarizing in a quintessential way the qualities and aspirations, styles and attitudes around him or, if he is more prescient, he expresses, before his contemporaries, the latent strivings that need only be expressed once to burst forth as new directions.

Carder was constantly attempting to develop new techniques, new formulas. Some of these paralleled efforts of his great contemporary Tiffany—indeed, in some cases, they appear to have followed those efforts. These two men were roughly of the same generation, had been exposed to the same forces, and, although at one point there was a confrontation, both, in retrospect, realized that the priority of an idea is a difficult thing to quantify.

For some thirty years Carder directed Steuben. Thousands of different forms were produced, hundreds of different colors and major compositional families developed. The variety and richness of his output have been superbly recorded in Paul V. Gardner's *The Glass of Frederick Carder*, and are perceptively discussed by him later in this book.

Despite a continual search to enlarge his vocabulary in the medium, Carder's work—including the latest pieces—reflects the late nineteenth and early twentieth centuries. Basically, it speaks with the strong voice of the past.

However important and valuable that voice is, there comes a time when it is no longer heard. Whatever its strength, it dims in the ears of those who are listening; its message, however valid, is rejected. The tendency is to ignore it and to start afresh. This is what happened with Steuben: An infinitely rich palette, an enormous vocabulary, had finally crushed creativity. And, as so often happens, a very young, inexperienced, but ambitious person perceived the fact and sought out completely new directions.

In 1933, Arthur A. Houghton, Jr., became president of the company. Bringing together a team of architects and artists, either as members of the Steuben staff or as consultants, he tossed out color and began to exploit a recently developed optical glass composition of unusual brilliance, which had splendid working properties.

To understand the significance of this development, we must turn to the past again, for the reaction manifested by Steuben's new direction—against rich colors and highly decorative surfaces—had already taken place abroad. Before World War I, Bohemia and Austria were developing new forms, sometimes rejecting color to emphasize engraving and the sparkle of the material. This trend was given further impetus near the end of the war, at Orrefors, in Sweden, where a staid old glass company was revitalized under the leadership of two ambitious young artists, Simon Gate and Edvard Hald. For them, too, one of the great virtues of glass was its brilliance, what it did to and with light, the fluid form swelling and contracting, in harmony with the engraved or sparingly cut design. The influence of this new vision was instantaneous, and for the next decades Orrefors and other important Swedish companies such as Kosta achieved prominence.

It is on this foundation that the new direction at Steuben was based. I hasten to say that this was not an imitative approach but, rather, reflected the realization that a new aesthetic was in formation. This new aesthetic found in Steuben one of its most articulate exponents in the Western Hemisphere. Indeed, a competitor, in the finest sense of the word, had emerged for the best work that was being done abroad.

The artists that Arthur Houghton drew around him rapidly produced forms that were entirely new in the history of glass. The design philosophy was based on total excellence. It was also based upon total control. This meant that the inclinations of the gaffer, the influences that he might have unwittingly contributed, were carefully subdued or eliminated. What was produced was a patrician glass for an increasingly patrician market. Exhibition followed exhibition, and series on various themes were created. World War II marked a period of consolidation that was followed by a tremendous outpouring of new ideas exploiting an ever more brilliant and technically perfect material.

Imagination there was in great measure, guided consistently by a distinct stylistic preference and furthered by a receptivity to experimentation in new forms—some daring, some geometric, some otherwise—that, to a hitherto unprecedented extent, exploited the optical properties of the material. These, however, were considered experiments, and only slowly did they have an impact on the mainstream of production.

Great emphasis was put upon "style," upon quality, upon excellence in every aspect of production, from the paper that wrapped the product, to the letterhead that billed it, to the case in which it was displayed, to the shop in which it was shown. All was carefully conceived and executed. A level of technical perfection which was virtually unheard of in the second half of the twentieth century was achieved.

Such a search for perfection, however, may lead toward sterility and even, in some cases, to meretriciousness; one may detect these characteristics in some of the later compositions, particularly those that include in their design gold and other precious materials. They are the unavoidable concomitant of a program aimed at satisfying, primarily, a wealthy market. This program was not closed to new directions, simply conservative. Under the impact of earlier experimentation and the infusion of younger points of view and talents, it is now undergoing change, and one cannot say with certainty where it will take the company during the next ten years. The panorama of accomplishment achieved under two completely different types of leadership, and the level of technical and, in some cases, artistic excellence that was reached in the 1950s and 1960s, however, augur well, not only for the survival of this unique company but for its making in the future—as it has in the past—a lasting contribution to design in general and to the history of glass in particular.

STEUBEN GLASS:
THE CARDER YEARS, 1903-32

PAUL V. GARDNER

Steuben's beginnings and its products prior to 1932 are relatively unfamiliar today. Until recently even more obscure has been the name of Frederick Carder (1863–1963), founder of the original Steuben Glass Works (after 1918, the Steuben Division of Corning Glass Works) and its guiding genius throughout the first third of the twentieth century. Carder was lured to America from his native England by Thomas G. Hawkes, president of T. G. Hawkes & Company, a Corning, New York, firm especially noted for its cut and engraved glass. Although this factory had been in operation since 1880, it had never manufactured the glass "blanks" which its artisans decorated; Hawkes offered Carder the opportunity of establishing a glass factory in Corning to produce blanks. Not only was Hawkes willing to arrange for most of the financial backing, but he also agreed to provide a building that could be readily converted to glassmaking. Carder, who since 1880, had been associated with the English glassmaking firm of Stevens & Williams, could supply the technical and artistic requirements and the ability to organize and run the factory. In this fortunate combination were the beginnings of Steuben.

From the start it was apparent that Carder's creative urge would not be satisfied by making glass to meet another firm's needs. Before the first Steuben blanks were in the hands of Hawkes's workmen, Carder was dreaming of the glass he would produce and offer for sale under Steuben's fleur-de-lis trademark. At the time Steuben was founded, colored glass was in demand on both sides of the Atlantic, and Art Nouveau was still in vogue. The late nineteenth-century innovative glass creations of Eugène Rousseau, Emile Gallé, Daum Frères, and others in Europe and the superb Favrile glass of Louis Comfort Tiffany in America had captured the luxury market and challenged competition. It is, therefore, not surprising that within a year Carder successfully completed his experimentation with a gold metallic luster glass, which he registered in the U.S. Patent Office as Aurene. This glass was an immediate success, and a year later he brought out its counterpart, Blue Aurene. Both of these were produced in considerable quantity during the years Carder was in charge of Steuben.

Gold and Blue are the only true Aurenes; pieces made from these glasses vary considerably in brilliance and color shading. The earliest Gold Aurenes, produced while the technique was still somewhat experimental, have a purplish cast. From about 1905 the fully developed color of Gold Aurene, a rich velvety lustrous gold, often with reddish shadings and radiating hair lines, is characteristic. This metallic luster surface was produced by spraying the Aurene glass (which contained salts of rare metals) "at the fire" with tin and/or iron chloride solutions under specially controlled atmospheric conditions (*Colorplate 1*). Blue Aurene also has subtle shadings throughout each piece, usually varying from dark blue to a pale silvery hue, although red-violet, greenish blue, and golden tones are also found occasionally (*Ill. 1*). As in the Gold Aurene, fine radiating lines appear on the rims or other areas that were expanded after the iridescent surface was developed. These lines are produced intentionally and do not appear on objects that were fully formed before being sprayed to produce the metallic luster surface.

Some of the more elegant Gold Aurene vases were ornamented by trailed decorations of leaves and vines in green glass, often enhanced with Millefiori accents (*Colorplate 1*). These were made in limited quantities during the first decade the factory was in operation and are now avidly sought by collectors.

Another important group, mostly vases and ornamental bowls made from about 1905 to 1910, are the so-called Red and Green Aurenes (*Ills. 2, 3*). These names are somewhat misleading as the only Aurene glass in these handsome pieces is the applied trailed and/or hooked decorations and the Gold Aurene linings and feet of some objects. The bodies of these pieces are usually Calcite or Alabaster either wholly or partially cased with ruby or green glass.

Verre de Soie, as its name suggests, is a lustrous glass having an iridescent silken sheen, usually heightened by a rainbowlike play of colors (*Ill. 4*). As with the Aurenes the lustrous surface was produced by a tin chloride spray "at the fire," and fine lines appear on the surface areas that were expanded after spraying. Produced throughout the Carder era, most Verre de Soie pieces were not decorated, although some were embellished with threadings, prunts, and other applied decorations in various colors, and a few have engraved patterns.

Although Carder produced no limited editions, some of the glass that displays several of his finest colors and techniques was made in relatively small quantities. Tyrian glass, made about 1916, is in this category (*Colorplate 2*). The pieces are of two color types: a pale bluish green produced when the glass was worked directly from the pot, and a bluish green, shading to bluish purple, produced when the glass was reheated to develop this special color effect. Most pieces were decorated with applied Gold Aurene leaves and trailed threads smoothed to the level of the glass, as well as "hooked" threadings in Gold Aurene and white, usually around the necks of vases. Trailed decorations in Aurene and other colors are also found on Alabaster jars and disks (*Ill. 5*).

Carder's voluminous sketchbooks document his years of systematic study at museums and private collections and reveal his almost reverential regard and appreciation for all fine glass. Whether it was made by ancient artisans or his competitors, every noteworthy piece of glass Carder saw challenged his artistic and technical ability. Carder's responses to many of these challenges are recorded in his Steuben productions. The scope of these productions overwhelms the historian and astounds the connoisseur. It is even more amazing that one man evolved the glass formulas, designed the forms and decorations, supervised the production, and dictated the sales policies of this complex establishment.

One response to the challenge of an ancient technique is Carder's Millefiori glass—made a few pieces at a time from about 1915 to the late 1920s (*Colorplate 4*). Inspired by Egyptian and Roman prototypes, these jewel-like vessels were fabricated from sections of glass rods which were first fused into a mosaic-like pattern and then formed into bowls, plates, and other shapes.

Even without seeing his sketchbooks, it is apparent that Venetian artisans had a marked influence on Carder's productions. Whether his homage to the Maestri di Murano took the form of a graceful covered vase surmounted by an elegant finial or an ovate water-lamp enhanced by elongated teardrops, it consistently proclaimed his admiration for the important Venetian contributions to the field of glassmaking (*Ills. 6, 7*).

A group of vases and bowls that Carder named Grotesque provides a delightful contrast to his classical designs (*Ill. 8*). These free-flowing forms, no two of which are exactly alike, were usually made in crystal at the base, shading upward to deep blue, ruby, and other transparent colors. Heavy ribs support the sides, allowing the thinner glass between to undulate freely. These pieces were put into production about 1929 or 1930.

The sometimes flamboyant effects produced by incorporating crushed or powdered glass of various colors into glass objects have intrigued glassmakers of many cultures. A successful version of this traditional technique is Steuben's Cintra, which was made by "picking up" crushed colored glass on a molten glass matrix and enclosing the whole in a casing of crystal (*Ill. 9*). Care was taken to perform these manipulations in such a way that relatively few minute bubbles were visible in the finished object, a characteristic that distinguishes Cintra from other Steuben glasses featuring bubbles as part of the decoration.

When bubbles were wanted to enhance the decorative effect, as in Cluthra, they were induced by mixing a chemical with the crushed glass (*Ill. 10*). Steuben's powdered glass components varied from coarse granules or fragments to the finest particles, called "frost." The coarser types were made by crushing heavy blown glass bubbles or fragments from Steuben rejects. The frost was obtained by pulverizing specially blown thin-walled glass spheres. The layer, or casing, of crystal that usually covered the powdered inclusion varied in thickness according to the effect desired. In most of the Cintra and Cluthra pieces, the casing is relatively thin, acting as binder to hold the colored glass fragments more firmly in place and to enhance the optical effect. In special pieces, such as the massive cologne bottles, the heavy casing became a featured element of the design, sheathing the glowing Cintra center in prismatic crystal, often highlighted with controlled bubbles (*Colorplate 5*).

Carder also relied on powdered glass to give the characteristic pattern to Moss Agate pieces, which was usually combined with a crackle effect and occasionally a few sizable bubbles. As in the Cintra and Cluthra pieces, the transparent glass casing provides an added touch of elegance (*Ill. 11*).

Amethyst Quartz featured another use of the powdered glass technique (*Ill. 12*). Amethyst colored frost and threads were "picked up" on a crackled glass matrix and enclosed in a crystal glass casing. Tooled floral decorations and feet in crystal were added to some pieces. After cooling, the surface was etched, usually in a floral design, and the entire piece given a mat or satin finish with buffed highlights. Quartz effects were also produced in rose, blue, green, peach, yellow, and alabaster.

Although Carder was not fond of cut glass, particularly heavy cut crystal, he bowed to public demand, and Steuben produced cut glass tableware and ornamental pieces in considerable quantities. During the first ten or fifteen years of the firm's history, "brilliant period" designs predominated. After this style went out of fashion, much of the cutting on stemware, table ornaments, and other decorative pieces was done in combination with engraving (*Ills. 13, 14*).

Engraved decorations to Carder's designs were done by local engravers in their home studios, using the copper-wheel technique. The designs were either left in mat texture as they came from the wheel or polished in the "rock crystal" style. Floral motifs predominated, but fish, human forms, crests, and other designs were used as desired. When cut motifs were combined with the engraved patterns, they tended to strengthen the design and accent the delicacy of the engraving.

Many of the more elaborate table services were made in Carder's crystal, usually cased with gold-ruby, green, blue, or amethyst, although other colors were also used. The designs were cut and engraved through the outer colored layer and appeared in mat or polished crystal against the colored ground.

Table services designed exclusively for individual customers were frequently made (*Ill. 15*). These usually combined the family coat of arms, crest, or personal monogram with a specially designed pattern engraved and/or cut on one of the standard production forms. Special shapes in stemware could be had, but use of the standard forms lowered the initial cost and facilitated replacement. These elegant services often included eight or ten types of drinking glass selected from as many as twenty available forms and ranging from graceful stemmed goblets to sturdier highball and whisky tumblers. In addition, candlesticks, center bowls, compôtes, finger bowls, and sherbets, as well as cigarette holders, plates, and a wide variety of other useful and ornamental pieces, could be ordered.

Acid-etched pieces reached the height of their popularity in the 1920s. Vases, bowls, and lighting fixtures were the principal types produced, but tableware was also made. Most etched vases were of cased glass, usually with a darker colored glass covering a lighter inner layer (*Color-plate 3, Ill. 16*). A large number of color combinations were used; Gold or

Blue Aurene cased over Alabaster, Pomona Green, or Jade Yellow were some of the more successful. Monochrome etched pieces were also produced, as were occasional three-layered combinations made in order to obtain a special color effect, as in Plum Jade (*Ill. 17*).

The names Carder gave his special glasses and decorative patterns range from the obvious and unimaginative to the farfetched and enigmatic. Aurene, one of the earliest, was coined from the first three letters of *aurum*, the Latin word for gold, combined with the last three letters of *schene*, the Middle English form of *sheen*, which describes the gold luster of the glass. Tyrian's purple overtones suggested to Carder the imperial purple fabrics of ancient Tyre, but the origin of Cluthra's name was lost even to Carder; in later years he could only suggest it meant "cloudy." One name that seemed to hold a unique place in Carder's esteem was Intarsia. Derived from the Italian term for inlaid woodwork, Intarsia designates at least three totally different types of Steuben glass. The first two types were made prior to about 1915, but the third, produced somewhat later, is by far the most important; indeed, Carder considered it to be his greatest achievement in artistic glassmaking (*Colorplate 6, Ill. 18*). By means of an extremely difficult production technique, a design in colored glass was enclosed between two thin layers of crystal. Usually the three layers have a total thickness of less than one-eighth of an inch. Although Carder experimented with this technique as early as 1916, no commercial productions were made before 1920 or 1921. A few of these early pieces were exhibited at the Metropolitan Museum of Art in 1925. Most of this glass was made in the late 1920s and early 1930s. No record of the number produced is available, and less than one hundred of these are known at present. All those produced for sale have a facsimile signature, "Fred'k Carder," engraved on the piece, usually on the side of the vase or bowl.

The glass objects mentioned here represent only a sampling of the intricate techniques and myriad colors of the Carder years. Even those who do not applaud all of Carder's designs concede that he had a superb technical mastery of the glass medium. Time will give the final evaluation of his achievements, but a consistently increasing appreciation of his accomplishments has already placed the Steuben creations of Frederick Carder in the top echelon of early twentieth-century American glass.

1. *BLUE AURENE*
Designed by Frederick Carder

Left to right:

Vase, 1905
Height: 6 inches
Unmarked
Collection of the Corning Museum of Glass

Vase, 1920s
Height: 8 inches
Mark: late signature* "Aurene F. Carder"
Rockwell Collection, Corning, New York

Pair of cologne bottles with flower stoppers, ca. 1930
Height: 6¾ inches
Mark: both have late signature "Aurene F. Carder"
Private Collection

Blue Aurene is made by the same basic glass formula as Gold
Aurene, with cobalt oxide added to give the blue color. Very few Blue
Aurene pieces are decorated, as Carder felt the subtle shadings of
this glass needed no embellishment. However, some early pieces are
decorated. The vase on the left, which has a feather-type hooked
decoration, is one of these. It bears the date 1905 in wax pencil in
Carder's handwriting. Others have trailed and/or Millefiori decorations. A few Blue Aurene pieces with various forms of decoration
appear from time to time. In the 1920s, four Steuben vase shapes
with applied horizontal trailings and leaves in white glass were made
in limited quantities.

The vase in the center and pair of colognes on the right are examples of the Blue Aurene color range and luster variations, which
continued to make this glass popular throughout Carder's regime.

* Marks denoted as "late signatures" were added by Carder to factory-made pieces
generally in the late 1950s and early 1960s. They do not indicate that the piece was
made by Carder but that it was his design, made at Steuben or occasionally at
Stevens & Williams. This is not true of his lost-wax castings, made after Carder left
Steuben. These were all made by Carder, and most are signed and dated.

2. *VASE* ca. *1905–10*
   Red Aurene
   Designed by Frederick Carder
   Height: 10 inches
   Mark: "Aurene 296," late signature "F. Carder"
   Rockwell Collection, Corning, New York

Red Aurene is the name used in Steuben catalogues to describe a special group of decorative pieces, usually vases, of Alabaster or Calcite glass partially or wholly cased with ruby glass, and having applied Aurene decorations on the outer surface. Many of these pieces also have Aurene linings and/or borders, and a few solid ruby pieces with Aurene trailings and/or Millefiori decorations are also called Red Aurene. This name, which is somewhat confusing, probably evolved as a shortened description of these objects in the factory and was eventually used throughout the Steuben organization to denote these rare pieces.

3. *VASE, ca. 1905–10*
   Green Aurene
   Designed by Frederick Carder
   Height: 7 inches
   Mark: "Aurene 606"
   Rockwell Collection, Corning, New York

Green Aurene is the factory name applied to green glass objects and Alabaster or Calcite glass pieces partially or wholly cased in green glass with applied Aurene decorations and/or linings. As with Red Aurene, the only Aurene glass in these pieces is the linings and trailed decorations.

4. *BOWL, ca. 1916*
   Verre de Soie with turquoise glass prunts and applied threadings
   Designed by Frederick Carder
   Diameter: 10½ inches
   Unmarked
   Collection of the Smithsonian Institution, Washington, D.C.

When this glass was introduced early in Steuben's operation it was called Flint Iridescent—an accurate description, as this glass is lead crystal (often called flint in nineteenth-century England and America) with a rainbow iridescence produced by a stannous chloride spray "at the fire." Under the more romantic name Verre de Soie, it became a Steuben standard and continued in demand for three decades.

8. *VASE, early 1930s*
   Grotesque style
   Designed by Frederick Carder
   Height: 9 inches
   Mark: late signature "F. Carder Steuben"
   Rockwell Collection, Corning, New York

The fanciful styling of these vases and their companion bowls demonstrates Carder's ability to depart occasionally and delightfully from the restrained, classical forms he loved so consistently. In calling these pieces Grotesque, Carder may have wished to emphasize the contrast between them and the more traditional Steuben forms.

9. *VASE*, ca. *1917*
   Cintra technique in pink and blue stripes with black applied decora-
   tions on neck and shoulders
   Designed by Frederick Carder
   Height: 9½ inches
   Mark: late signature "Fred'k Carder"
   Collection of the Corning Museum of Glass

Cintra pieces were made by "picking up" crushed and powdered colored glasses on the parison (molten gather of glass) and forming
them into the desired shapes, usually with an added layer of crystal
to enclose and suspend the partially fused particles. Although both
controlled and random bubbles are often included in the heavy crystal casings, the thinner Cintra pieces are usually without noticeable
bubbles or with bubbles so small they are inconspicuous. Cintra
pieces were made in monochromes, shaded colors, and vertical
stripes of alternating colors like this vase, which Carder kept in his
private collection for nearly half a century. He prized it as one of
the finest examples of his Cintra technique. Although he made Cintra
at least as early as 1917, there is no indication as to how much was
sold at that time. Carder was known to rename a variation of a
standard color when its popularity began to wane, and there is a
possibility he may have called a variation of striped Cintra by the
name Or Verre at a later date in order to stimulate sales. A 1921
trade journal records the introduction of a new Steuben color called
Or Verre but gives no description of this glass, and a Steuben cata-
logue shows a line drawing of a vase of the same shape as this one
with a notation, "Or Verre." But up to the present time this color has
not been positively identified.

10. *PILGRIM BOTTLE or VASE, ca. 1930*
   Cluthra technique in green shaded to white with crystal handles and
   outer casing
   Designed by Frederick Carder
   Height: 10 inches
   Unmarked
   Rockwell Collection, Corning, New York

Cluthra has been described as Cintra with bubbles. This oversimplified definition, which points out the most obvious difference between these similar glasses, should be supplemented with the other generalizations that most Cluthra is made with coarser glass particles and a heavier crystal casing than Cintra. (Notable exceptions are the massive Cintra pieces with very thick crystal casings such as the cologne bottle shown in Colorplate 5.) Carder felt bubbles gave life to the glass, and he included them intentionally in many of his pieces whenever he felt they enhanced the design. He said the random bubbles of various sizes in Cluthra were produced by mixing a "chemical" (probably potassium nitrate) with the powdered glass on the "marver," or surface on which the glass from the pot is rolled to make it smooth. This "chemical" reacted to the heat of the parison, forming the myriad of bubbles featured in Cluthra pieces. It was necessary to cover the rapidly forming bubbles with a casing of crystal and contain them at the moment when they reached the desired size and density. This urgency combined with the pleasing optical effect was a dual reason for the heavier crystal casing on Cluthra.

11. *VASE, 1920s*
   Moss Agate. Rare blue matrix with crackle
   Designed by Frederick Carder
   Height: 15 inches
   Unmarked
   Collection of David Williams

Moss Agate pieces may have the same form but are never duplicates, as the powdered glass inclusions never produce exactly the same pattern. All Steuben Moss Agate is rare, but, as the majority of these pieces are predominantly in shades of red, brown, and yellow, the blue matrix of this vase with its variegated blue, purple, black, and green shadings indicates a most unusual and perhaps unique piece. In Carder's unpublished manuscript "Glass and Glassmaking as I Know It" (1920) he says: "In the case of Moss Agate, it is then crackled on the inside by inserting a tube of brass or iron perforated with fine holes and connected to a water supply. This must be done quickly and the surplus water emptied out of the vase or other object and then reheated in the glory hole so that the cracks will not go too far through the walls." This reheating unites the shattered pieces perfectly but leaves the attractive netlike crackle pattern.

12. *BOWL or VASE, ca. 1930*
    Amethyst Quartz glass with applied and etched decorations. Satin finished with buffed highlights
    Designed by Frederick Carder
    Height: 7 inches
    Mark: Acid-etched fleur-de-lis in relief (almost illegible)
    Collection of Dr. and Mrs. L. G. Wagner

This rare bowl demonstrates a combination of several glassmaking techniques. The mottled amethyst color is from powdered glass "picked up" from the marver in the same technique as that used in producing Cintra pieces. The leaves and feet are of crystal applied "at the fire," and are tooled while the glass is still hot to give the effect of veinings and bark. After the piece is annealed, the floral design in low relief is acid-etched and the entire surface and applied decorations given a satin finish with buffed highlights.

Colorplate 1

While still in England, Carder was intrigued by the beauty of Roman iridescent glass and experimented for years with the production of a metallic luster glass that would simulate the rich, lustrous effects of these ancient pieces. Within a year after he founded Steuben, Carder perfected the glass formula and production technique for making this glass, which he called Aurene—a name he coined from the first three letters of *aurum*, the Latin word for gold, and the last three letters of *schene*, the Middle English form of *sheen*. This name now seems doubly significant, as it not only describes the appearance of the glass but also symbolizes the Roman inspiration and the English origin.

The purplish color of the small vase on the right indicates an early experimental piece made before the full rich tones of Gold Aurene were fully perfected. The disk shows the fully developed Gold Aurene color, which combines the gold- and rose-colored tones produced by the tin and iron chloride sprays "at the fire." The radiating lines are intentional and are produced when the glass is manipulated and expanded after spraying. The metallic coating precipitated on the surface of the glass does not stretch with the expanding glass and separates, leaving the fine lines between the metallic fragments.

The rare Gold Aurene vase in the center is decorated with thin Millefiori cane sections, which form the white flowers surrounded with leaves and trailed threadings of green glass. Most of the pieces of this style were produced during the first decade the factory was in operation.

Colorplate 2

VASE, 1917
Tyrian with trailed decorations in Gold Aurene
Designed by Frederick Carder
Height: 10½ inches
Mark: "Tyrian, F. Carder 1917"
Collection of the Corning Museum of Glass

The purple shading of this rare Steuben glass was developed by re-heating "at the fire." When not subjected to this reheating operation, the entire glass object remains a pastel green color, similar to that on the neck of the vase. The applied leaves and trailed threadings are of Aurene glass, which is reheated and smoothed to the surface level of the vase. Carder considered this vase one of the best Tyrian pieces made during the short time this glass was in production—about 1916–17. He kept it in his private collection until his death in 1963, when it was bequeathed to his daughter, Gladys Carder Welles, who gave it to the Corning Museum of Glass in 1969.

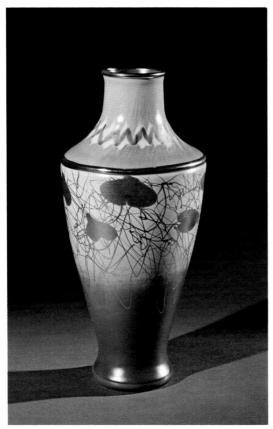

2

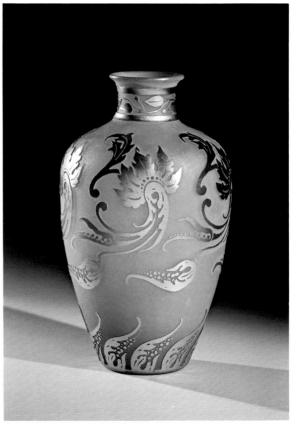

3

4

6

Colorplate 3

VASE, probably late 1920s
Blue Aurene cased over Jade Yellow with etched decoration
Designed by Frederick Carder
Height: 8½ inches
Mark: late signature "Aurene F. Carder"
Collection of the Corning Museum of Glass

This handsome vase with its acid-etched design in Blue Aurene cased over Jade Yellow illustrates how the inner casing affects the color of the outer layer. The Jade Yellow backing accents the silver sheen in the upper units of the design and lightens considerably the blue shadings of the motifs at the base. For many years this rare vase was in the Welles Collection (Mrs. Welles was Frederick Carder's daughter). It was bequeathed to the Corning Museum of Glass in 1969 by the Welles estate.

Colorplate 4

BOWL, probably made between 1915 and the early 1920s
Millefiori
Designed by Frederick Carder
Diameter: 6¼ inches
Unmarked
Collection of the Corning Public Library

Millefiori ("thousand flowers") is the name given by Venetian glass-makers of the Renaissance to their revival of an ancient glassmaking technique dating at least as early as the third century B.C. This bowl, following the style of these ancient pieces, is made from sections of Millefiori glass rods arranged in a mosaic-style pattern in a mold, fused together, and then formed into a hemispherical bowl finished by a heavy thread around the upper rim. Carder's rare Millefiori pieces are made in both mat (satin) and bright finishes.

Colorplate 5

COLOGNE BOTTLE, ca. 1928
Blue and pink Cintra center cased in heavy crystal with controlled
bubbles and cut decoration
Designed by Frederick Carder
Height: 11½ inches
Unmarked
Collection of the Smithsonian Institution, Washington, D.C.

The vibrant pinks and blues in the Cintra glass center of this massive cologne bottle are partially veiled by the network of controlled bubbles and enhanced by the depth of the crystal casing. Broad panel and facet cuttings on the outer surface create a prismatic illusion which is heightened by a kaleidoscopic play of colors as the piece is viewed from various angles. Very few of these bottles were produced, and all differ in form, the color of the Cintra core, the pattern of the included bubbles, and type of surface cutting. This piece is probably unique.

Colorplate 6

VASE, ca. 1930
Intarsia with design in blue glass between two layers of crystal
Designed by Frederick Carder
Height: 6½ inches
Engraved facsimile signature: "Fred'k Carder"
Private Collection

Carder considered Intarsia his finest achievement in artistic glassmaking. Although Carder did no actual glassblowing at Steuben, he spent endless hours in the blowing room coaching the gaffers. When a complicated technique such as the Intarsia baffled the glassworkers, Carder would advise, cajole, and "cuss" the gaffers until the desired result was achieved. Fewer than 100 Intarsia pieces are known and all are unique. This limited production was due to the complicated technique involved in the blowing room, the lack of understanding of this difficult technique by the average viewer, and the introduction of these special pieces in the depths of the 1930s Depression, when sales of all luxury goods were at their lowest ebb. Most Intarsia pieces are vases and bowls, but a few stemware items were also made. The colored design is usually in shades of amethyst, blue, green, and occasionally black. In some pieces, the black glass layer is so thin it appears as a grayish blue. All but a few experimental bowls and stemware pieces bear the engraved facsimile signature "Fred'k Carder."

13. *LUMINOR or TABLE ORNAMENT, late 1920s*
Crystal pigeon with cut decorations
Designed by Frederick Carder
Height: 6 inches
Mark: "Steuben" (block-letter acid stamp)
Collection of the Smithsonian Institution, Washington, D.C.

In addition to the pigeon, cut crystal eagle, pheasant, duck, and pea-
cock table ornaments were made. These objects were among the few
Carder Steuben pieces in which the basic shape was formed in a
mold and the feathers and other details added by the glass cutters
after the piece was annealed. The bird alone was used as a table
ornament. When placed on a square box of black glass containing an
electric light, the bird was illuminated from beneath and used as a
luminor, or night light.

14. *COVERED BOWL*, ca. *1928*
    Moonlight glass with cut decorations
    Designed by Frederick Carder
    Height: 14¾ inches
    Unmarked
    Collection of the Smithsonian Institution, Washington, D.C.

The delicate tint of this rare color varies from a pale grayish blue in daylight to a pinkish gray and other shadings when seen by artificial light, depending on the source. The polished, cut floral motifs and border V-cuts are accented by the "gray" (unpolished) random "gang cuts," which form the decorative background.

15. *PART OF A TABLE SERVICE, 1920s*
   Gold ruby cased over crystal with engraved and cut decoration spe-
   cially designed by Frederick Carder for L. P. Fisher
   Large plate diameter 14 inches
   Mark: "Steuben" (block-letter acid stamp) on most pieces
   Rockwell Collection, Corning, New York

Up to the present time we have been unable to determine how many
pieces were in the original order for this service. We know that each
place setting consisted of at least six different stemware items plus
highball glasses, finger bowls, plates, and dessert plates. These pieces
were generally ordered in lots of a dozen or more of each item and
usually also included sherbets with plates and other matching acces-
sories. The large plate and candlesticks shown in the photograph
were often supplemented with compôtes of various sizes and a
footed center bowl for fruit or flowers. Note the "LPF" monogram
that appears as part of the engraved design on each piece.

16. *VASE*, ca. *1932*
     Gold Aurene cased over Alabaster. Acid-etched decoration in Winton pattern
     Designed by Frederick Carder
     Height: 8 inches
     Mark: late signature "F. Carder Aurene" (faint)
     Collection of Mr. and Mrs. Marvin Hosier

This etched decoration in Art Deco style is an indication of Carder's ability to follow a current trend. It was one of the designs selected to be produced for a year or so after Carder was transferred from the Steuben Division and made art director of the Corning Glass Works. Note the absence of the fine hairlines in the Gold Aurene casing, which indicates the vase was fully formed before the stannous chloride spray was applied.

17. *BOWL, late 1920s*
Plum Jade glass. Acid-etched decoration in Canton pattern
Designed by Frederick Carder
Diameter: 8 inches
Rockwell Collection, Corning, New York

The unusual color of this bowl depends on a combination of three layers of glass—two amethyst layers separated by a layer of Alabaster. To achieve this double casing, the Alabaster and amethyst glasses must have the same coefficient of expansion. If these layers or casings do not expand and contract in unison the object will shatter. The acid-etched design is confined to the outer amethyst casing and is called a double-etched pattern because there are two steps involved in its production. First, the main design motifs are printed in wax "ink" on the outer surface of the bowl. The bowl is dipped in acid and etched to the desired depth (about halfway through the outer amethyst casing). Second, the scroll-type background is printed in wax "ink" on the etched background around the main motifs, which are still protected by the original wax coating. The bowl is then dipped again in the acid and the spaces around the scrolls etched away until only a thin layer of the amethyst outer casing remains. The wax is then removed and the design appears in three shades of amethyst. The middle casing of Alabaster backed by the inner casing of amethyst brings out the contrasting shadings of the etched design, which vary in intensity from piece to piece, and greatly enhances the overall color effect.

18. *BOWL*, ca. *1930*
    Intarsia with design in amethyst glass between two layers of crystal
    Designed by Frederick Carder
    Height: 4 inches
    Engraved facsimile signature: "Fred'k Carder"
    Collection of the Corning Museum of Glass

As with the other Intarsia pieces of this type, the design is a thin layer of colored glass enclosed between two layers of crystal. In this bowl the floral design is in pale amethyst. The facsimile signature is engraved on the lower exterior of the bowl.

STEUBEN GLASS:
THE HOUGHTON YEARS, 1933-73

JAMES S. PLAUT

In 1933, the directors of the Corning Glass Works were considering liquidation of the company's Steuben Division. Arthur A. Houghton, Jr., the youngest member of the Corning Board and a great-grandson of Corning's founder, went before his fellow directors to ask that he be given control of the Steuben Division. The division had been formed at the end of World War I and had an indifferent business record in spite of Frederick Carder's creative genius. In Houghton's mind, the division's weakness was that it held to no definable style of glassmaking but—in the tradition of all things to all men—produced many different kinds of glass and distributed its wares haphazardly through the country's department stores and gift shops.

Arthur Houghton wanted to explore the potentialities of fine glassmaking by Corning. A young Harvard graduate and already an avid collector of rare books, he had high cultural goals, both for himself and for his family's company. The Corning Board, which had suffered steady losses by the Steuben Division for many years, gave Houghton a free hand in its reorganization. In the autumn of 1933, Steuben Glass, Inc., was formed as a new company. Houghton became its chief executive officer and Corning Glass Works its sole stockholder. Houghton asked the young architect John M. Gates, his friend and contemporary, to join him as Steuben's design leader. Gates, in turn, invited Sidney Waugh, a sculptor, to become the new Steuben's first designer. It is noteworthy that all three men were still in their twenties.

Houghton considers, in retrospect, that only their youth and inexperience made it possible for them to approach the Corning Board with the proposition that "with the small group of skilled workmen and the pure crystal glass that we have, with a little capital, a little time and a free rein, we will try to make the finest glass in the world."

Two rather simple factors governed the newly formed company's philosophy. First, for centuries design had been entrusted primarily to the glassmaker himself, and, generally, the more experienced he was, the more lavish and complex were his creations. Extravagance, rather than discipline, was the hallmark of the seasoned maker. Therefore, Houghton, Gates, and Waugh set about to plan Steuben's design program consciously and cogently. Second, during Corning's evolution of over 50,000 different formulations of glass, a chemical formula for crystal had been discovered (in 1932), giving rise to the conviction that a crystal glass of matchless purity and transparency could now be produced.

From these considerations came Houghton's "Steuben Trilogy," which he described to Gates as follows: "The Trilogy embraces material, workmanship, and design. If any of these three elements is deficient, perfect glass cannot be achieved." This doctrine for Steuben's development also stipulated that the three elements be given equal prominence and be held in conscious balance.

One other factor in the creation of Steuben's new image was a fresh approach to the marketing of its products. Whereas the old Steuben had been sold indiscriminately to a large, heterogeneous variety of outlets, Houghton decided that the new Steuben glass would be sold only through its own shop on Fifth Avenue in New York, in Corning, and through controlled Steuben shops in a few high-quality stores. Eventually, Steuben shops were established in important metropolitan areas of the country.

Within a very short time, Steuben came to be regarded internationally as *the* American glass and the rival of the celebrated twentieth-century glass of Europe—made by Baccarat and Lalique of France, Venini of Italy, Lobmeyr of Austria, and Orrefors of Sweden.

At Steuben the material itself—the Steuben Trilogy notwithstanding— has always been the dominant element. The firm has cited laboratory tests that establish its glass as comparable to fused quartz or pure rock crystal. Steuben has a high index of refraction compared to conventional glasses, and this contributes to its high reflective quality. The purity of the crystal, coupled with a refined melting process, results in a metal free of seeds, cords, and other imperfections. The tone of Steuben's development during the forty years of Houghton's stewardship was set by the company's constant desire to make the best possible use of this superb material. Steuben has also taken great pride in its workmen who, surrounded by the sophisticated technology practiced by Corning in industrial production, make Steuben glass by the off-hand process, as glass has been made for hundreds of years. Robert J. Leavy, who was in charge of production for many years, including the crucial period of transition when Steuben changed from colored glass to the present transparent crystal, worked with four generations of glassworkers. Most of the first generation were trained in Czechoslovakia, England, Germany, and other traditional centers of glassmaking. The chief glassblower, or "gaffer," John Jansson, for example, came from Sweden, where he had studied with his father, a master glassworker before him. Jansson and his brother Siegfried, who also worked as gaffer at Corning for many years, are typical of the Steuben corps of glassworkers—now and yesterday—men cast in the same mold, quiet, painstaking master artisans, superbly skilled in the techniques of craftsmanship. Today, an increasing number of Steuben's glassworkers are natives of Corning, trained in local schools and on the factory floor.

As with the glassworkers, so with the men who engrave the glass. The Hungarian-born Joseph Libisch came to America early in the century after apprenticeships in Vienna and Prague, and in 1921 embarked on a long career at Steuben. Today, in training programs initiated by Leavy, Libisch's successors impart to their colleagues the wisdom and artistry gained through seventy years of activity in the leading ateliers of two continents. The painstaking arts of copper-wheel and diamond-point engraving as they are practiced at Steuben Glass can be observed by all visitors to the factory at the Corning Glass Center. Basic methods have not changed in the last 350 years. An eighteenth-century engraver would feel quite at home with the twentieth-century glass-engraving equipment at the present Steuben factory.

Steuben's insistence over the years on the purest crystal, fashioned by the hands of skillful craftsmen, was no guarantee per se of distinguished glass. The history of glass provides all too many tasteless nonentities that happen to have been made well and of excellent material. Clearly, if good material is the foundation, and good workmanship the force, then design must dictate the form which the whole will assume.

Throughout the Houghton era, Steuben's designers faced both the opportunities offered and the limitations imposed by a specific material. Whereas, under Frederick Carder, Steuben shone resplendent in all the colors of the rainbow, Houghton's glass was absolutely colorless, depriving his designers of a broad range of options in surface treatment and subtle combinations of hue and tone. At first, the mood was pure and austere. Indeed, luxury and ornateness were long in coming. The first works produced under Houghton were simple and massive, with some looking over the shoulder—it now seems—at the excellent glass produced in Sweden in the 1920s. Steuben's tableware of the 1930s—glasses and tumblers, bowls and candlesticks—created an enduring impression of weight and value. The early pieces were more utilitarian than decorative, but the stamp of elegance was already upon them.

In due course, the limpid metal became embellished. In 1935 Sidney Waugh designed the rhythmic, engraved *Gazelle Bowl* (*Colorplate 7*), which became the first in a long series of decorative pieces marking his contribution to Steuben over several decades and culminating in the rich *Merry-Go-Round Bowl* of 1947 (*Ill. 40*). Waugh died in 1963, having participated with Houghton and Gates in the formation of Steuben Glass, having given early direction to its design, and, probably more than anyone else, having perfected a form of art which led in time to the frequent selection of Steuben glass as his country's official presentation gift.

Steuben Glass existed for less than a decade before its operations were disrupted by the nation's involvement in World War II. The company did not regain full momentum until the late forties. Whereas the production of useful pieces continued unabated, Steuben was now moving steadily in the direction of larger, more ambitious examples of the glassmaker's art. A series of special exhibitions and special projects had provided added incentives for the creative team. As early as 1935, the Knoedler Gallery exhibited Steuben concurrently in New York and London. In 1937, the Gold Medal of the Paris Exposition was received. In 1939 and 1940 Steuben exhibited at the San Francisco Golden Gate International Exposition and New York World's Fair and, throughout the late thirties, at a number of American museums.

In 1937 Gates met Henri Matisse in Paris. After Matisse had volunteered to make a drawing to be engraved on a Steuben piece, Gates commissioned drawings from an eminent group of European and American painters and sculptors. "Design in Glass by Twenty-seven Contemporary Artists" was the first of many Steuben projects undertaken with the objective of unifying the arts and demonstrating the useful collaboration of artists and artisans.

In 1951 Steuben was invited by the French government to present a special collection at the Musée des Arts Décoratifs in Paris. Steuben was the only American glass represented in an exhibition of European glassmaking, and the collection was given central prominence. The Steuben group contained 28 pieces incorporating designs by French and American artists, and 134 other works.

For Steuben, the fifties became a period of great and diverse activity, during which the company came of age in virtuosity and reputation. President Truman, and then President Eisenhower, established the tradition of presenting Steuben glass to other heads of state, and a series of major ceremonial pieces was produced for Presidential presentation to France, Great Britain, Norway, and the Soviet Union, as well as the Vatican and the United Nations. Steuben glass is now represented in the state collections of more than seventy countries.

The fifties also witnessed a series of special projects conceived by Arthur Houghton and his associates that gave Steuben repeated opportunities to scan the world and seek designs from a considerable number of artists of international stature. "British Artists in Crystal" of 1954 embraced designs by twenty painters and sculptors, including Jacob Epstein, Graham Sutherland, John Piper, and John Nash.

During 1954 and 1955, Steuben commissioned a series of designs from artists throughout the Near and Far East with the help of Karl Kup of the New York Public Library. In January 1956, "Asian Artists in Crystal" was opened by Secretary of State Dulles at the National Gallery of Art in Washington. It was shown later at the Metropolitan Museum of Art in New York, and then went on tour to the sixteen countries whose artists had contributed to the collection.

The growing tendency at Steuben to produce major ornamental pieces was accented in 1959 by a group of thirty-one "collector's pieces" in engraved crystal, representing the work of Steuben's own designers— Waugh, George Thompson, Donald Pollard, Don Wier, and Lloyd Atkins. By the end of the fifties, Steuben had developed a corps of designers whose strength and versatility were sufficient to bring to a halt the company's intermittent reliance upon outside artists. The work of the sixties and seventies, with only rare exceptions, has been by members of the Steuben design staff.

In 1963, Houghton made a singular excursion into the world of "the related arts," attempting on this occasion to use poetry for inspiration. Commissioning works by thirty-one poets selected by the Poetry Society of America, Houghton challenged Steuben's designers to capture in crystal the mood of the poems. Conrad Aiken, W. H. Auden, Robinson Jeffers, Marianne Moore, Richard Wilbur, and William Carlos Williams were among the poets whose works were chosen for this effort.

"Poetry in Crystal" initiated another new development—Steuben's marriage during the sixties of glass with precious metals, commencing with a design by Donald Pollard. Later, many pieces combining glass and metal came from the fertile imagination of James Houston, who joined the Steuben design team in 1962 after spending twelve years with the Eskimos in the Canadian Arctic as an educator and administrator. Houston's *Trout and Fly* (*Colorplate 9*) reveals the love of nature that he expresses in a number of descriptive pieces, and illustrates Steuben's own exploration of the aesthetic gains to be realized by combining its shining crystal glass with rich metals.

Houghton was not entirely pleased with the program he had initiated. "I believe," he said, "that we should not permit these objects of glass and metal to represent more than a fraction of our overall effort. We are *glassmakers*, not goldsmiths or jewelers, so glass must always predominate with us; and we must learn to combine glass with other materials in a more sophisticated way." Yet the desire to combine glass with precious metals persisted throughout the sixties, culminating in a few elaborate, one-of-a-kind *objets d'art* where engraved crystal is embellished with gold. These highly ornate pieces are superb technically, and surely represent the epitome of twentieth-century glass engraving. Each has been purchased by a private collector at a price equivalent to that of a major work of art.

Steuben's steady thrust toward objects of greater virtuosity did not proceed entirely from the experience and skills accumulated over several decades of glassmaking. Although Houghton aspired constantly to perfect a higher art form, there was also, as he explains, an underlying economic rationale:

> We found out some time ago that our functional objects could not possibly be made to compete in the market with other products. I have to think of the survival of our company and the welfare of its employees—over 250 people. We have had to seek new ways to utilize our resources—each pound of glass, each skilled man hour of blowing-room or engraving time. There is a subtle balance between what it costs to make a piece and what price you can command for it. We have been a rather proud family in Steuben, and we have worked together well. I have always wanted to guide the company's policies so as never to let these people down.

Retrospective analysis suggests that the sixties also brought to Steuben a contrasting but perhaps more permanently valid tendency, the probing search for new forms and new uses. To be sure, experimentation has always been a Steuben hallmark, and it must be recalled that the vast commercial gains registered over the years by Corning Glass, Steuben's parent company, are due largely to the reinvestment of its resources in long-term research and development. (It has long been Corning's policy to allocate a high percentage of its profits to the investigation of new methods and applications of glass manufacture.)

Paul Schulze came to Steuben as a designer in 1961 and was appointed director of design in 1970, following the retirement of John Gates. "My aim," says Schulze, "is to let glass speak for itself in all its beautiful clarity. I am interested in the material and what it does. I am always looking for new adventures in the technology of glass." Contrast this statement with the design philosophy of Schulze's colleague James Houston, the artist, writer, and naturalist. "I am interested in having the glass *say* something to you. You look and you respond because you know *what it is*. My glass has to tell a story. I am not interested in abstract forms and I could never do them."

But other gifted associates could. As early as 1955, George Thompson, Steuben's accomplished senior designer, had contributed *Sea Breeze*, (*Ill. 51*), a composite of flowing sculptural forms; and Donald Pollard's *Genesis* (*Ill. 54*) is an abstract, ovoid sculpture enhanced by delicate engraved tracery. Schulze has pressed hard for new forms and new directions. His *Prismatic Column* (*Ill. 61*) and *Quintessence* (*Colorplate 12*), utilizing new methods of cutting and decorating, are adventures in glass that parallel the flow of the major arts of our time.

Thus it is that Steuben, for almost two decades, has sought separate and parallel goals in glassmaking: on the one hand, opulence and enrichment, utilizing historical, literary, and figurative devices; on the other, diligent study of the material itself and the attempt to capture its essence in new ways. Schulze approves of this duality of approach, recognizing that "a company seeking to widen its markets without sacrifice of excellence must offer its public an increasingly broad choice."

What, then, is the special ethos of the Houghton years? His contributions were diverse: first, the vision and courage to start a new enterprise based on personal conviction; second, his insistence upon the use of a gloriously beautiful material and his staunch refusal to permit any deviation from it toward other kinds of glass; third, his fierce ambition to make Steuben *the* American glass, without peer; fourth, his laudable desire to use Steuben as a vehicle for the creative unification of the major artistic resources of his time; fifth, but by no means last, his awareness that any business enterprise must be viable, since consistent financial losses would erode the creative effort and lead ultimately to Steuben's extinction.

Arthur Houghton has always had a penchant for elegance, luxury, and tradition. He has not been friendly to the avant-garde, and his tastes in art have not favored the experimental leaders of this century. He seems always to have been enchanted by ceremony and the color of pageantry. Yet it was the sheer *adventure* of Steuben that stirred him most deeply. Whatever his personal tastes, he encouraged experimentation and protected its exponents. With unquenchable vigor he proposed project after project to his Steuben associates and prodded them relentlessly toward new and changing achievements.

Although his leadership of Steuben over forty years was absolute, Houghton said recently, "It would be wishful thinking on my part to imagine that Steuben would always go on being what I would like it to be, and I don't even want it that way. The future Steuben will carry the image of its leadership exactly as it has during my years." Arthur Houghton retired at the end of 1972 and the moment of his prophecy is now at hand.

Assessment of the arts of one's own time is a frustrating exercise, inescapably subjective and necessarily inconclusive. The passage of time provides needed perspectives and comfortably separates the wheat from the chaff. It would be altogether too simple, therefore, to praise or condemn Steuben for its adherence to (or departure from) the major currents of twentieth-century art. During the Houghton years, Steuben had its share of admirers and detractors, those who collected it avidly and those who avoided it assiduously.

What I believe about Steuben is this: When future students of twentieth-century American culture examine the artifacts of our time and the society that produced them, Steuben will receive high marks. No doubt it will be judged to have been made to delight the elite rather than to satisfy a popular need; but it will not be indicted for this, since the arts of the Roman Empire, the Renaissance, and the eighteenth century, for instance, were also thoroughly elitist.

I also believe that future historians will grant to Steuben the fashioning of a significant new American art glass if not a new American art form, and in this distinction Arthur Houghton (looking down quizzically from above) will probably be disappointed. One suspects that Steuben will be regarded not only as having provided satisfaction for a segment of an affluent society but, in an important sense, as having taken its place in the great continuum of glassmaking that began with the Phoenicians. Indeed, Steuben's major pieces, displayed in the Metropolitan and Victoria and Albert museums of the future, will have much in common with the Cellinis, the Fabergés, and the exquisite German glass of the seventeenth century.

Presumably, Houghton's Steuben will be judged to have been a phenomenon of luxury and elegance, standing well outside the mainstream of twentieth-century art, so much of which is spare and austere.

Examining Steuben's relationship to its gigantic sponsor, the Corning Glass Works, historians may express surprise that the child drew so little from the incredible technical prowess of the parent. Yet Corning's technology has been utilized essentially for the production of functional glass, in massive quantities and by highly automated methods, so that very few of Corning's technical applications lend themselves to the painstaking manufacture of glass by hand. One is more affected, perhaps, by the anomaly of Corning's housing Steuben—Corning, whose commitment to research leads to the future, Steuben, which looks to the past rather than ahead for assurance. While this disparity in *esprit* may startle the observer, it is appealing to know that Corning, in the role of patron, nurtures what appears to be an incongruous pattern of coexistence. From one point of view, of course, Steuben is the shining cap of the Corning iceberg. As such, it not only lends luster to the whole enterprise, but suggests that Corning makes just about *everything* in glass.

As to Steuben's future, Paul Schulze says, "We are on the threshold of exciting breakthroughs in the making of fine glass that are the result of an intimate, constructive and inventive relationship of all the creative forces at our disposal. We think the horizons are unlimited, and the only thing we will always insist upon is absolute truth to the material itself."

There is further promise. Arthur Houghton says, "the taste and discernment of my successor will be the controlling factor." Houghton's successor, who assumed Steuben's presidency early in 1973, is Thomas S. Buechner, a man of imposing credentials, an accomplished museum director, scholar, critic, author, and painter. Buechner has grown up and lived *within* the arts of our time. He knows the trials and the glories of creativity from firsthand experience. He is superbly equipped to lead Steuben into the future. Buechner says:

I knew Fred Carder for more than a decade. I have known Arthur Houghton since 1950. Carder could do anything with glass—trained as an artist and technically the most innovative glassmaker of his time, he was a one-man band. Houghton, on the other hand, is a patron of the arts in the grandest sense—a pragmatic, planning philosopher who has made base glass as prized as precious metal. Such awesome predecessors make prediction presumptuous. I plan to maintain the extraordinary quality of Steuben crystal and of Steuben craftsmanship; new designs will reflect these unique qualities and an awareness of our potential in this most venerable and suddenly most contemporary of aesthetic media.

19. *TABLE GLASS, 1934*
Designed by Frederick Carder

One of the Carder designs that were carried over into the Houghton years, each of these goblets is "a glassmaker's piece of glass," in the words of Robert J. Leavy. He recalls: "We had a stem-maker named Otto Johnson, and he made from twelve to fifteen of these goblets in an hour—one every five minutes—and he made each one of these glasses in *one heat*. The problem here is the straw stem; the trick is to keep the thin stem straight as it's warmed into the bowl of the goblet. If you give it more than one heat, the stem collapses. A speedy art! If you've got a man like Johnson, you've really got a glassworker."

Certain manipulations are fundamental to the making of all blown glass. Most stemware produced by the "off-hand" method includes, among other things, the following basic steps, as detailed in *The Making of Fine Glass* by Sidney Waugh (New York: Dodd, Mead, 1947):

"First, a 'gather' of molten glass is taken from the furnace by dipping the blowing iron into the molten metal. The gather is then rotated in a wooden forming block to give it uniformity of character. The glass is blown to form a bubble.

"From another iron or pontil, another gather is dropped onto the blown shape to form the stem of the goblet. The stem is tooled to its final shape and another gather of glass is dropped onto the stem to form the foot.

"A pontil is then attached to the foot, the goblet is cracked off from the blowing iron with a touch of a cold pincer and the whole piece is now reversed on the arms of the workbench. The excess glass is sheared off, a puff of compressed air expands the bowl of the goblet to its proper size and the bowl is opened out and brought to its final shape.

"The blowing of the goblet is now complete, and it will be carried to the lehr for annealing."

The tallest goblet illustrated, with an engraved monogram, is shown in the exhibition.

20. *ZODIAC BOWL, 1935*
    Designed by Sidney Waugh
    Diameter: 16 inches
    *Collection of The Art Institute of Chicago, Gift of Mr. and Mrs. Hugh
    J. Smith, Jr.*

A crystal bowl, a blown form opened out into a shallow bowl, engraved with the twelve signs of the zodiac in clockwise order around
the rim, this work followed soon after the successful *Gazelle Bowl*.
The *Zodiac Bowl* is also in the collections of the Metropolitan Museum of Art, New York, and the Victoria and Albert Museum, London. The *Zodiac Bowl* was first engraved by Joseph Libisch.

In the 1930s, before Sidney Waugh became Steuben's associate
designer, engravers did not do much figure work; they were pre-
occupied instead with natural forms, fruit, flowers, coats of arms,
etc. Engravers at that time did their work at home. To obtain the
desired standard and style in figure work, and to form an association of these artisans within the factory alongside the glassworkers,
the engravers moved at this time to workbenches at Steuben.

21. *MASSIVE CUT VASE, 1935*
Designed by Sidney Waugh
Height: 11 inches
Collection of The Metropolitan Museum of Art, Fund of Edward C. Moore, 1935

One of the first forms designed by Sidney Waugh for Steuben, the vase consists of two separate blown forms that are fused together. The piece is then cut to the artist's specifications and polished.

22. *HIGHBALL GLASS, 1937*
Height: 4½ inches

This drinking glass of generous proportions requires a fine glass-blower indeed to produce the desired thickness at the base and then the transition to a thinner edge at the top, which creates a subtle optical effect.

24. *TEARDROP CANDLESTICKS, 1937*
Designed by F. B. Sellew
Height: 9 inches

"The ultimate in glassmaking," in the words of Robert J. Leavy. Making this candlestick requires a five-man shop on the blowing room floor: the gaffer, the servitor, two bit-gatherers, and a carry-in boy. First, the servitor blows the base; two bits are added to make up the stem. This is given to the gaffer, who puts on the candle-cup that he has meanwhile formed. The foot is then opened out by the gaffer, who then finishes off the cup at the top. When the center section is formed, a small blow is put into the glass to form the bubble.

Colorplate 7

GAZELLE BOWL, 1935
Designed by Sidney Waugh
Diameter: 6½ inches
Collection of the Metropolitan Museum of Art, Fund of Edward C.
Moore, 1935

The first engraved piece designed for Steuben by the sculptor Sidney Waugh, the *Gazelle Bowl* is blown of clear crystal and rests on a solid crystal base cut into four flanges. It is engraved with a decorative frieze of twelve leaping gazelles. Now one of Steuben's classic designs, it was first engraved by Joseph Libisch. The *Gazelle Bowl* has been commissioned more than fifty times.

Sidney Waugh (1904–63) was Steuben's first chief associate designer. He, with Arthur A. Houghton, Jr., and John M. Gates, was responsible for Steuben's new direction in design taken in 1933. Trained as a sculptor, Sidney Waugh was awarded the Prix de Rome in 1929. His work is represented in collections of museums in the United States, Latin America, and Europe. President of the National Sculpture Society, and director of the Rinehart School of Sculpture in Baltimore from 1942 to 1957, Sidney Waugh was the author of two books, *The Art of Glassmaking* (New York: Dodd, Mead, 1938) and *The Making of Fine Glass.*

The master engraver Joseph Libisch taught many other Steuben engravers. Steuben's vice president for production Robert J. Leavy realized in the 1930s that the factory needed a nucleus of young engravers. A training and apprenticeship program was then set up to carry on the art Libisch brought to Corning from Europe in the early years of the century.

The *Gazelle Bowl* is also in the collection of the San Antonio Art League, the Smithsonian Institution, Washington, D.C., the Toledo Museum of Art, the Indianapolis Museum of Art, the Cummer Gallery of Art, Jacksonville, Florida, and the Museum of Ceramics and Glass, Kuskowa, U.S.S.R.

MOBY DICK, 1959
Glass design by Donald Pollard
Engraving design by Sidney Waugh
Length: 11¼ inches

An interpretation of the struggle between Captain Ahab and the white whale in Melville's novel *Moby Dick*. The entire form is cut from a block of crystal. Following the shape of the crystal, the whale is engraved as a shadowy mass on the far side. In the foreground, the thickness of the crystal giving an illusion of intervening space, is engraved a longboat with Captain Ahab and crew in the final attack.

   Moby Dick was first engraved by Kenneth Van Etten.

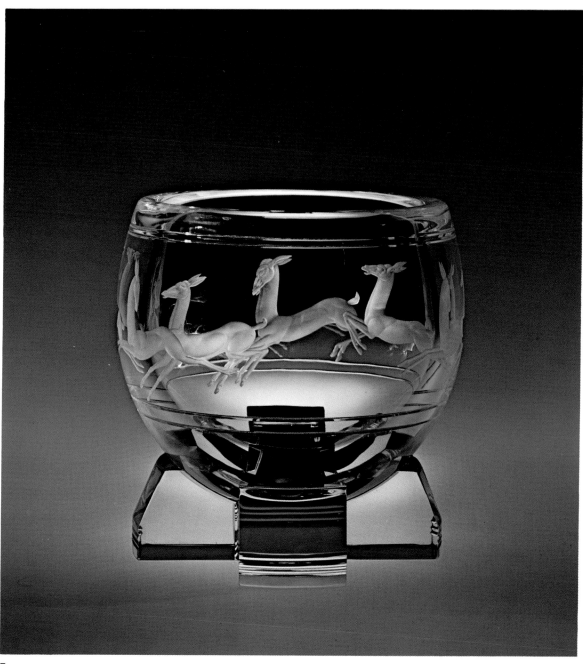

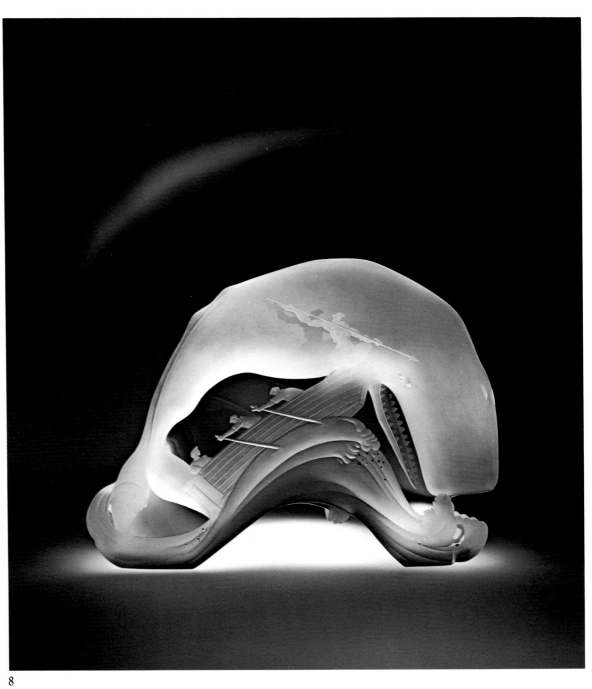

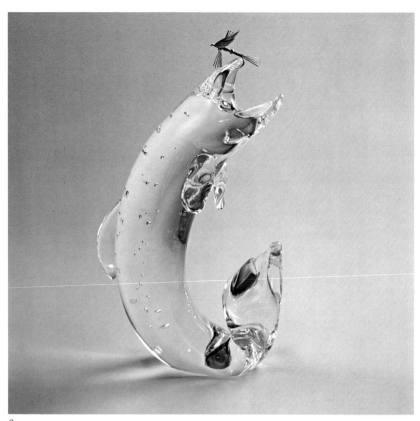

9

10

Colorplate 9

TROUT AND FLY, 1966
Designed by James Houston
Height: 9½ inches

Trout and Fly was one of the first Steuben pieces in which crystal and precious metal were combined (the fly is eighteen-karat gold). The body of the fish is a "covered" piece of glass, the bubbles created by making indentations in the first shape in a prescribed pattern so that, when the second layer covers them, air is trapped to form a bubble pattern. The fly is a Royal Coachman.

Colorplate 10

CUT VASE, 1969
Designed by Paul Schulze
Height: 6½ inches
Collection of Milton R. Friedberg

Made in the round with the slender opening blown in from the top, the piece of crystal is then cut and polished into irregular facets.

THE GREAT RING OF CANADA, 1967
Designed by Donald Pollard
Engraving design by Alexander Seidel
Engraved by Roland Erlacher and Ladislav Havlik
Height: 40 inches
Collection of the Government of Canada

"For the People of Canada on the Centenary of Canada's Nationhood from the People of the United States of America," *The Great Ring of Canada* was presented in 1967 to Prime Minister Lester Pearson by President Lyndon B. Johnson. It is a unique piece.

The Great Ring of Canada symbolizes the nation and the individual components that comprise it. Held in a setting of rhodium-plated steel, a great ring of cut and engraved crystal plaques is surmounted by a smaller ring of crystal and a finial of faceted crystal spheres.

From a circular steel base, twelve slender steel arms branch out to hold the ring of twelve large, emerald-cut crystal plaques. The plaques are engraved with the armorial bearings and flowers of the ten provinces and two territories of Canada: Alberta, British Columbia, Manitoba, New Brunswick, Newfoundland, Northwest Territories, Nova Scotia, Ontario, Prince Edward Island, Quebec, Saskatchewan, and Yukon Territory.

Above the great ring the twelve arms converge. A smaller ring of crystal stands free from and encircles them. Here are mounted four crystal plaques, two engraved with the arms of Canada, and two with a natural maple leaf enclosed in the formal Maple Leaf of the Canadian flag. The smaller ring is engraved in each quadrant with the motto of Canada: *"A Mari Usque Ad Mare"* ("From sea to sea").

Rising above the second ring, the arms hold the finial, a circle of twelve faceted spheres symbolizing the provinces and territories, from whose center emerges a larger, many-faceted sphere symbolizing the nation they together form.

Inscribed around the rim of the steel base is the dedication.

25. *COCKTAIL GLASS, 1944*
Designed by George Thompson
Height: 3¾ inches

This glass with air-twist stem is shaped by the glassmaker in three steps: first the bowl is blown; then the air-twist stem is attached; finally the foot is added. The air-twist spiral is made in advance by grooving a gather of glass and then covering it over with another layer of glass, so that parallel tunnels of air are trapped within the glass. The whole is then twisted (the tunnels wrap around each other in a spiral) and pulled out like taffy to reduce the diameter. Stems, as required, are then cut off from the resulting rod.

26. *BOWL, 1939*
Designed by Walter Heintze
Diameter: 13½ inches
Collection of Mr. and Mrs. James A. Thurston

After a heavy-walled bubble is formed, the top or rim of the bowl is "cupped-in" with a tool. Forcing the heavy wall into a tight curve gives the bowl a shining inner surface.

The designer, Walter Heintze, came to Steuben from Sweden.

27. *ROPE-TWIST CANDLESTICKS, 1939*
Designed by George Thompson
Height: 8 inches
Collection of Mrs. Lambert R. Walker

These objects, almost Art Deco in feeling, are formed simply by taking hot glass, crimping or grooving it, drawing it out, and twisting it to form the stem to which the base and cup are added.

32. *THE CAT, 1940*
   Engraving design by Isamu Noguchi
   Diameter: 10 inches
   Collection of The Columbus Gallery of Fine Arts, Columbus, Ohio,
   Gift of Mrs. Sallie Jones Sexton in memory of her parents, Mr. and
   Mrs. John Sutphin Jones

This piece of clear crystal, a blown form opened up into a plate, is decorated with the linear engraving of a cat, drawn by the distinguished artist Isamu Noguchi. Noguchi's original brush drawing, in ink, is here faithfully interpreted. This plate, engraved by Peter Schelling, was issued in an edition of six.

The Cat was one of the "Designs in Glass by Twenty-seven Contemporary Artists," first shown in an exhibition by Steuben Glass in 1940. The exhibition originated when John M. Gates, Steuben's director of design, met Henri Matisse in Paris in 1937. The great French painter, struck with the artistic possibilities of glass, offered to make a drawing for Steuben, to be engraved in crystal. Thus encouraged, Gates commissioned drawings from a group of eminent European and American painters and sculptors. Some of the drawings submitted indicated the shape and character of the glass envisioned by the artist, but in most cases, as with *The Cat*, the conformity of form to decoration was entrusted to Steuben's own designers.

Isamu Noguchi, a native Californian of Irish-Scottish and Japanese descent, was raised in Japan from the age of two. He worked for Gutzon Borglum in New York and received Guggenheim fellowships to study in Paris with Brancusi. His autobiography, *A Sculptor's World* (New York: Harper and Row, 1968), relates his achievement in sculpture and theater design. Noguchi's work is represented in collections of the Metropolitan Museum of Art, New York, the Museum of Modern Art, New York, the Whitney Museum of American Art, New York, the Guggenheim Museum, New York, and many others.

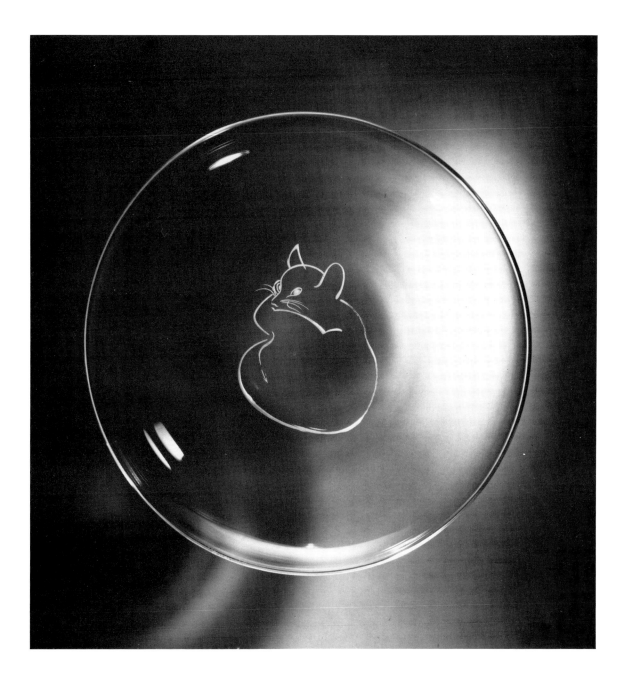

33. *ACROBATS, 1940*
   Engraving design by Pavel Tchelitchew
   Height: 13½ inches
   Collection of Mr. and Mrs. Harry W. Anderson, Atherton, California

Tchelitchew's first design for the medium of glass was commissioned as part of Steuben's continuing effort to explore possibilities for effective collaboration between artist and artisan. The renowned Russian artist was one of twenty-seven represented in Steuben's exhibition of contemporary work in 1940. Tchelitchew himself chose the crystal vase shaped like a giant brandy balloon for his circus scene.

   Acrobats, issued in an edition of five, was first engraved by Joseph Libisch.

34. *COCKTAIL GLASS, 1939*
    Designed by George Thompson
    Height: 4 inches

35. *COCKTAIL SHAKER, 1941*
    Designed by Donald Russell
    Height: 10¼ inches
    Collection of Mr. and Mrs. James A. Thurston

The cocktail glass is made in two parts. The base, when hot, is pierced with a tool, which sets in the air bubble. When the tool is withdrawn, the indentation is inflated by a puff of air to form the bubble, which is then sealed in with an added bit of hot glass. The bowl of the cocktail glass is then lined up with the base and the two are melded together.

The substantial cocktail shaker, the heaviness of which emphasizes the luster of the crystal, presents a special challenge in the finishing room: devising the exact fit of the stopper.

The designer, Donald Russell, a graduate in architecture of the Massachusetts Institute of Technology, joined Steuben's original design group in 1936 and remained with the company until his retirement in 1972. He designed displays and exhibitions and worked on plans for Steuben's regional shops throughout the country.

36. *THE VALOR CUP, 1940*
   Designed by John Monteith Gates
   Height: 15 inches
   Collection of John Monteith Gates

This tall covered urn blown of crystal rises from a pedestal base. Curving handles decorate the sides; the cover is surmounted by an ornamental finial composed of separate strips of crystal converging in a crownlike design. Engraved by copper wheel with the royal arms of Great Britain, *The Valor Cup* was presented to the British War Relief Society in commemoration of the Battle of Britain. (The piece in the exhibition is a replica.)

The Valor Cup was made by John Jansson and engraved by Joseph Libisch. To protect the delicate handles of the cup during the long engraving process, they were encased in plasticene.

The architect John Monteith Gates, Steuben's first director of design in the Houghton years, organized the Steuben design department in 1936, three years after the new company was formed.

Trained as an architect at Columbia University, Gates in 1933 won an international competition for the replanning of the central areas of Stockholm. In that same year, he joined Arthur A. Houghton, Jr., in the directorship of Steuben Glass, also becoming its chief of design. He retired in 1969. Gates was also director of design of Corning Glass Works, Steuben's parent company, where he was responsible for the design of most of the company's products, in addition to architecture, graphics, and packaging.

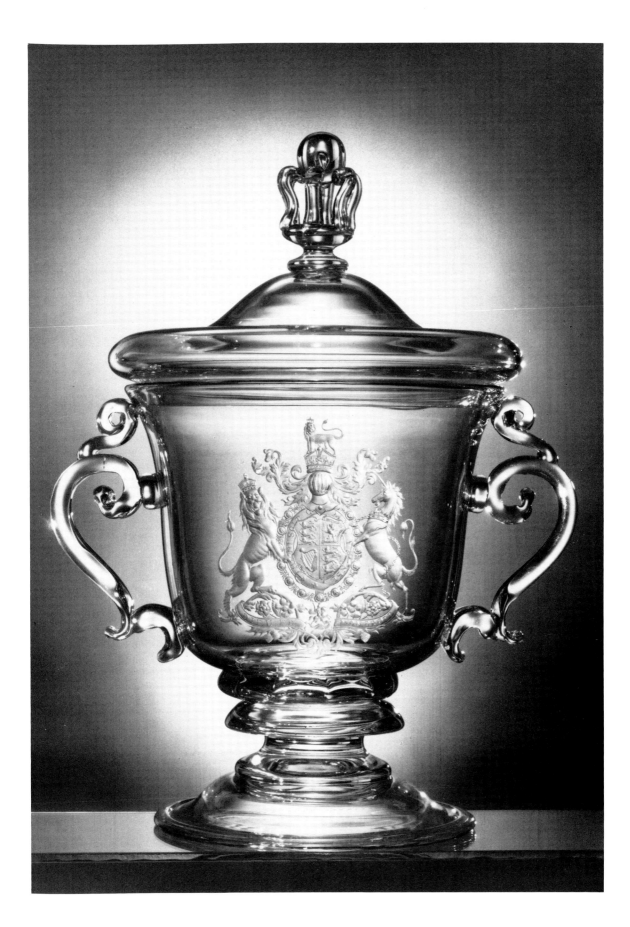

37. *SHIP'S DECANTER, 1942*
   Designed by Samuel Ayres
   Height: 10 inches

Contemporary version of a classic shape made to stand steady at sea, the *Ship's Decanter*, a blown form, is decorated with rings that wind around the neck, spaced to fit the hand when pouring. The glassworker's main problem is to be sure the bits of glass that form the rings meet precisely.

40. *MERRY-GO-ROUND BOWL, 1947*
Designed by Sidney Waugh
Height: 10 inches

Covered bowl with plumed finial and ornamental base, engraved to depict a carousel in motion. Both the body of the bowl and the top are blown and then matched so as to create an unbroken profile. The designer said of the piece, "The country fair is the oldest and most unaffected of our festivals, and the merry-go-round is the soul and symbol of that institution."

Engraved by Joseph Libisch, the *Merry-Go-Round Bowl* was presented to Her Royal Highness the Princess Elizabeth on the occasion of her marriage, November, 1947, by President and Mrs. Harry S. Truman. (The piece in the exhibition is a replica.)

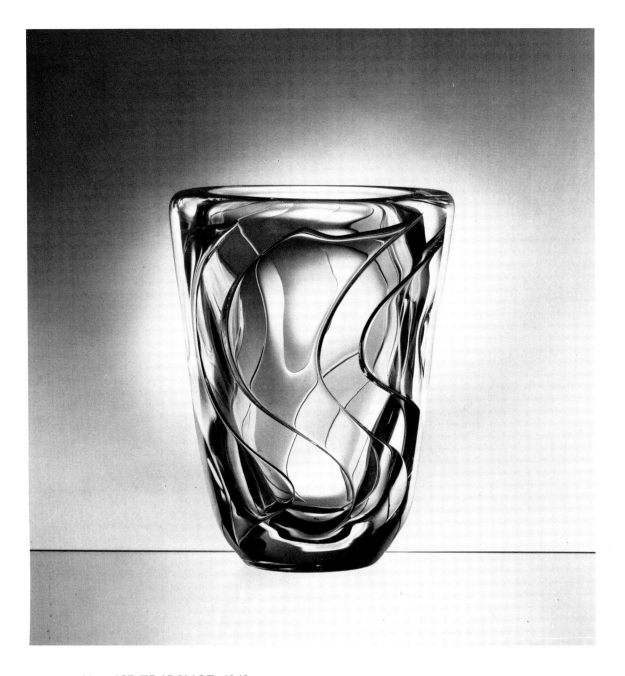

41. *AIR-TRAP VASE, 1948*
    Designed by John Dreves
    Height: 8½ inches
    Collection of The Metropolitan Museum of Art, Fund of Edward C.
    Moore, 1950

This massive crystal vase with decorative air traps is formed, first, by blowing a substantial bubble of glass and laying on strips of glass in a swirl pattern. A second, larger bubble is then produced and the first fitted in, as a hand in a glove. The spaces between the strips of glass give the resultant air-trap pattern.

Two of these vases were made.

42. *SNAIL, 1949*
Designed by David Hills
Length: 3¼ inches

Basically a scroll, this small decorative animal is made by a two-man
shop. While the gaffer or master glassmaker shapes the form off-
hand, the servitor gathers the bits that are added to the top of the
head.

43. *BUD VASE, 1949*
     Designed by David Hills
     Height: 8 inches

A slender object with air-trap base, the bud vase is made in two parts that are tooled together by hand. First, the body of the vase is blown. The base is pierced by a hot tool with a hemispherical tip to make the air bubble and then withdrawn. Another gather of glass is added to enclose the bubble and trap the air. The two parts are then indistinguishably sealed together.

The bud vase, which is also made with engraved inscriptions, was designed by David Hills, who studied industrial design at the Pratt Institute. He participated in the summer school Steuben set up in Corning, New York, in 1948, for young designers interested in glass, and remained with Steuben until 1952.

The bud vase is in the collection of the Cooper-Hewitt Museum of Decorative Arts and Design, Smithsonian Institution, New York.

44. *TABLE CRYSTAL WITH SPIRAL STEM, 1950*
Designed by George Thompson

The six pieces in this design are the goblet, champagne glass, and glasses for red wine, white wine, sherry, and liqueur. The fashioning of the air-twist stem is described in the caption for Illustration 25. Through the years, Steuben has made crystal plates, finger bowls, etc.

45. *TREFOIL BOWL, 1950*
Designed by Lloyd Atkins
Diameter: 6½ inches

The glassworkers at Steuben referred to this bowl for many years as the "silver dollar bowl," because of the size of the three bits, or pads, of glass that were laid on the base. The three bits shine like lenses and give added luster to the piece.

Lloyd Atkins, the designer, was born in Brooklyn, New York, and entered Pratt Institute in 1941. The next year he joined the United States Army Air Force. After World War II, he returned to Pratt, from which he was graduated with a Certificate of Industrial Design. In 1948, he became a member of the Steuben Glass design department, continuing his studies at night to earn a B.I.D. degree from Pratt. His work in crystal has been shown in many Steuben exhibitions, including those at the Louvre, Paris, Park Lane House, London, the National Gallery of Art, Washington, D.C., and the Metropolitan Museum of Art, New York.

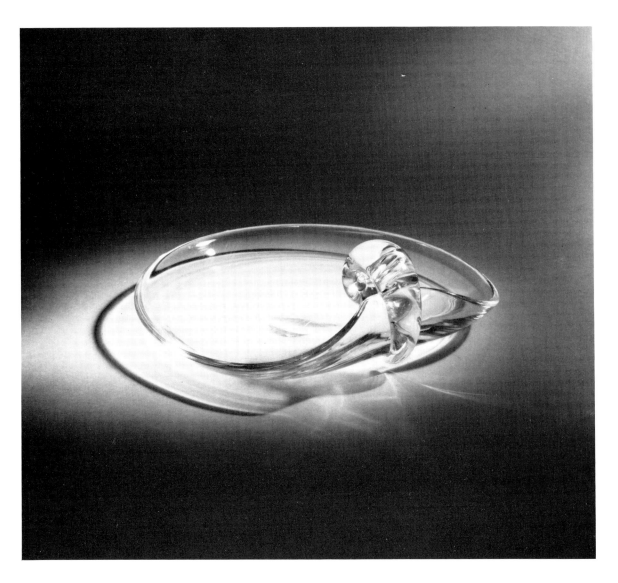

46. *SCROLL PLATE, 1952*
Designed by George Thompson
Diameter: 8 inches
Collection of Mr. and Mrs. Sterling P. Fisher

Designed for serving appetizers or candies, the *Scroll Plate* is formed by "lipping up" the basic shape after it is opened out. The bit-gatherer brings in a hot piece of glass, which is then formed to the desired scroll shape. The trick here is to have the right temperature for the bit and the right thickness for the bowl—both of which can be done only through experience.

The *Scroll Plate* is also in the collection of the Musées Royaux d'Art et d'Histoire, Brussels.

47. *SPIRAL BOWL, 1954*
Designed by Donald Pollard
Diameter: 7 inches

This versatile small bowl is embellished with a spiral base. Two
spirals are formed by dropping onto the sides of the bowl triangular
bits of glass that are drawn out and down into points. The bits seem
to emerge from the body of the bowl, go around the base, and
descend to the supporting surface.

Donald Pollard, designer and painter, a graduate of the Rhode
Island School of Design, became a staff designer for Steuben Glass
in 1950. Prior to joining Steuben, he participated in the trainee program of the Institute of Contemporary Art in Boston, working in
silver. He has also worked in the field of architectural theater design.
Pollard's pieces are represented in public and private collections
throughout the world, from the Metropolitan Museum of Art, New
York, to the National Gallery of Modern Art, New Delhi.

48. *ORCHIDS, 1954*
   Glass design by Donald Pollard
   Engraving design by Sir Jacob Epstein
   Diameter: 11 inches
   Collection of The Metropolitan Museum of Art, Gift of Udo M. Reinach, 1959

In 1954, Steuben organized its second exhibition of crystal produced by artists and artisans working in collaboration, "British Artists in Crystal." The object, according to John M. Gates, then Steuben's director of design, was "the creation of works of art in crystal where true artisans carry out the imaginative conceptions of great artists. In this particular medium, the result can be obtained only in collaboration, the one being dependent upon the other. The artists can scarcely learn the craft of glassmaking; nor can the glassmaker, absorbed in the long training of his profession, develop artistic mastery."

   Orchids, issued in an edition of six, was first engraved by Joseph Libisch.

49. *SPIRAL VASE, 1955*
Designed by Donald Pollard
Height: 6½ inches

After the vase has been blown and its narrow waist shaped, the bit-gatherer brings two triangular-shaped strips of glass that are laid on the base to form a spiral. The gaffer then opens the top of the vase by shearing. The bits add luster to the object as applied decoration.

50. *OWL, 1955*
Designed by Donald Pollard
Height: 5 inches

Made in the round by the glassworker, the owl shape is composed of two simple, solid forms. After it is carefully inspected for any tiny bubbles or inclusions that might mar its clarity, it is sent to the cutting shop. The beak is made with a small V-cut. The eyes are ground in and left with a mat finish; they are then polished in the center, and the engraver adds the pupils.

123

The *Owl* is in the collection of the Charles H. MacNider Museum, Mason City, Iowa, and the Children's Museum, Detroit Public Schools, Detroit, Michigan.

51. *SEA BREEZE, 1955*
Designed by George Thompson
Height: 14½ inches

These free sculptural forms of crystal suggest a wind-filled sail seen at a distance over the curve of ocean waves. Made of three separate pieces stoppered together, the solid basic shapes are formed off-hand in the blowing room. They are then refined by cutting, grinding, and polishing.

52. *SAYING OF CONFUCIUS, 1956*
Glass design by Donald Pollard
Engraving design by Cho Chung-yung
Height: 7 ¼ inches

This crystal stele has a Confucian inscription in formal Chinese calligraphy. The inscription reads from top to bottom, right to left, "Confucius said, 'Advance the upright and set aside the crooked, then the people will acquiesce.'" The lefthand column includes in smaller characters, reading from top to bottom, the artist's name, "written by," and the artist's seals. The rocklike form recalls stone slabs on which the followers of Confucius inscribed his words for posterity after earlier versions of parchment and silk had proved perishable.

Saying of Confucius was one of the pieces commissioned in 1954 by Steuben Glass to form a collection of work by Asian artists. Working with drawings by contemporary artists of the Far and Near East who were interested in this collaboration, Steuben's designers fashioned a group of pieces that made up the exhibition "Asian Artists in Crystal," first shown at the National Gallery of Art, Washington, D.C., and the Metropolitan Museum of Art, New York, in 1956, and then taken on an extensive tour of the Far and Near East under the auspices of the United States Information Agency.

Cho Chung-yung, the venerated calligrapher who wrote "Saying of Confucius" in formal Chinese characters, said of his own work, "I studied the nine fundamental brushstrokes when I was very young, and I have practiced and practiced. Your writing will be your best judge."

Saying of Confucius is in the collection of the Cooper-Hewitt Museum of Decorative Arts and Design, Smithsonian Institution, New York, the Metropolitan Museum of Art, New York, the University of Connecticut, Storrs, and the National Historical Museum of the Republic of China, Taipei, Taiwan.

53. *WHIRLPOOL VASE, 1958*
Designed by Donald Pollard
Height: 11 inches

Three bits of hot glass, triangular in cross-section, are wound around
the narrowing waist of the vase to give movement and reflection to
the piece.

Sidney Waugh, in an introduction to *The Making of Fine Glass,*
wrote, "In general it can be said that the secondary forms of an
object in glass should be somewhat heavier than in an opaque
medium. Small forms tend to disappear because of transparency.
For the same reason, all curves should be firm and robust. Because
of the essential beauty of the material, glass, like silver or porcelain,
is seen at its best when the forms are not overelaborated."

54. *GENESIS, 1959*
   Glass design by Donald Pollard
   Engraving design by Terry Haass
   Height: 11 inches

The solid crystal, ovoid form suggests the beginning of Creation, as described in the Book of Genesis: "And God said, Let there be light: and there was light. And God saw the light, that it was good: and God divided the light from the darkness."

Raised on the front surface of the glass is a planet-like sphere. The back is cut to give an effect of light in space. Swirling lines engraved on the piece represent the movement of planetary bodies. *Genesis* was presented to His Excellency Juscelino Kubitschek, President of Brazil, by President Dwight D. Eisenhower on the occasion of his visit to Brazil, in February, 1960. (A replica is shown in the exhibition.)

Genesis was engraved by Roger Keagle.

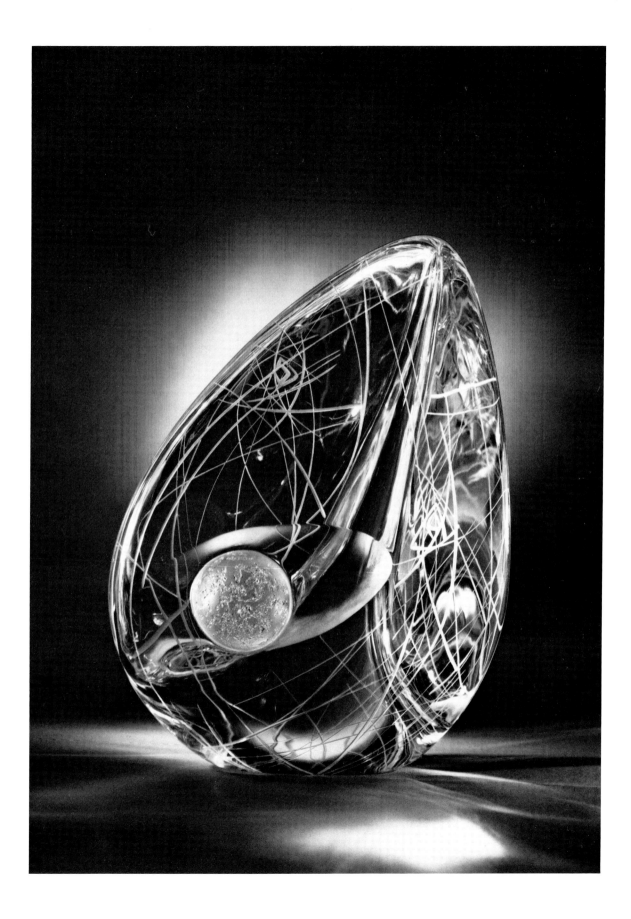

55. *PEONY BOWL, 1960*
Designed by Donald Pollard
Diameter: 12¾ inches

This wide crystal bowl is made in two parts. The solid round base is made by the gaffer, who adds to it the eight bits of glass. The servitor has meanwhile blown the bowl. These two parts are then joined together and the base is opened up.

56. *GRECIAN URN, 1962*
Glass design by Donald Pollard
Engraving design by Sidney Waugh
Height: 6½ inches

This crystal urn, a blown form, is an adaptation of a classic Greek krater, engraved to interpret the "Ode on a Grecian Urn" of John Keats. Engraved by Roland Erlacher, *Grecian Urn* is another of the designs by Sidney Waugh that established the art of fine engraved crystal in the United States.

57. *THE CERTAINTY, 1963*
   Glass design by Donald Pollard
   Engraving design by Dale Joe
   Width: 8 inches

This work illustrates a poem by John Holmes commissioned by Steuben Glass for the collection, "Poetry in Crystal." The poem begins:

> Though I ignore my geological past
> As if out of sight is out of mind,
> I have remembered the water-table
> That under all, not far down, never
> To be seen by man, we live or die of.

The designer, Donald Pollard, wished to reflect the water-table of the poem in his design. He conceived of two rugged, solid crystal forms, one set on top of the other to form a mirror image at the center. This mirror, representing the earth's water-table, reflects engraved streams of water flowing endlessly into and from the unpolished, rocklike forms at the edge of the piece.

The Certainty, issued in an edition of twelve, was first engraved by Ladislav Havlik.

Colorplate 12

QUINTESSENCE, 1971
Glass design by Paul Schulze
Gold design by Patricia Davidson
Diameter: 8 inches

Quintessence is a crystal and gold sphere formed of twelve glass cones, their apexes centered, and fifty gold rods, some with spiked, others with seed-pod finials. The piece was issued in an edition of five, one of which was presented to the Shah of Iran on the occasion of the 2,500th anniversary of the Persian Empire.

Patricia Davidson, co-author of *Greek Gold Jewelry from the Age of Alexander* (Brooklyn Museum, 1965), is a goldsmith who has done extensive research into ancient goldsmithing techniques. She is a research associate in the Brooklyn Museum's Department of Ancient Art.

Colorplate 13

PANELED OBELISKS, 1973
Designed by Lloyd Atkins
Height: 14¾ inches

These obelisks were cut from crystal blocks. Each obelisk rises in four successively smaller tiers separated by horizontal bands of double-bevel cutting. They were issued in an edition of five sets.

Colorplate 14

CUBED SPHERE, 1969
Designed by Paul Schulze
Height, with base: 6 inches

A cubed sphere of clear crystal encloses a sphere of bubbles. The bubbles are not produced by taking the glass in the usual way—as a gather from the melting furnace—but by letting the molten metal flow in a stream into a cup. The stream of hot glass overlaps in the cup, creating little air traps to form the inclusions seen in the center of the piece. When the cup is filled and a sphere with bubbles has been formed, this piece is covered over with clear crystal with no inclusions. It is then cut on six sides to form a cube with rounded corners. The crystal rests on a base of stainless steel.

13

14

Colorplate 15

TRIANGLES, 1971
Designed by Rush Dougherty
Height, with base: 6 inches

Cut from a single block of crystal, *Triangles* shows the interaction created by connecting parts of isosceles triangles cut on opposing sides of a transparent cube. The piece rests on a turntable of black leather.

Rush Dougherty joined the design staff of Steuben Glass in 1971. A graduate of Parsons School of Design, he has studied at the American College in Paris and the University of Strasbourg. Currently, Dougherty is concentrating on a series of geometric forms and variations in Steuben crystal. He is also involved in designing and mounting such Steuben exhibits as "Studies in Crystal," which appeared at the Corning Glass Center during the summer of 1971.

Colorplate 16

DANDELIONS, 1973
Glass design by Paul Schulze
Engraving design by Donald Crowley
Width: 7¾ inches

Contrasting forms are juxtaposed, as organic growth is viewed through a geometric solid. A dandelion cluster, its four shoots progressing from bud to seed-head, is engraved in an irregular crystal prism. The image is refracted so that, as the position of the viewer changes, the plant appears to divide and multiply.

Dandelions was first engraved, with copper wheel and diamond point, by Kenneth Van Etten.

141

58. *PORPOISES, 1964*
Designed by Lloyd Atkins
Lengths: 6, 9¼, 12 inches

The glassworker fashions the leaping porpoises from hot glass. After the nose and body of the porpoises are made, the object is "stuck up" on a pontil at the other end, toward the nose, so that the tail can be made. The mark of contact the pontil has made with the glass is afterward ground and polished away.

59. *EAGLE, 1964*
Designed by James Houston
Width: 12 inches

This four-part, solid form endeavors by the shape and luster of the wings to suggest the eagle's flight upward from the base.

The artist and writer James Houston joined the design department of Steuben Glass in 1962. He studied painting and the graphic arts in his native Canada, and in Paris and Tokyo. His works are represented in the collections of the Montreal Museum of Fine Arts and the Allied Arts Museum in Calgary, as well as many private collections. Formerly civil administrator for the Canadian Government in the eastern Arctic, he was instrumental in promoting exhibitions of Eskimo art throughout the world. He has written and illustrated five books, including his novel *The White Dawn*.

60. *CUT TOTEM, 1965*
Designed by Paul Schulze
Height, with base: 20 inches
Collection of Mr. and Mrs. Harry Breslau

The basic undulating shape is formed in the blowing room, of solid crystal. The column is then cut on four sides. It is mounted on a base of polished aluminum. This is a unique piece.

Paul Schulze, director of design for Steuben since 1970, joined the design department in 1961. He is a graduate of New York University and Parsons School of Design, where he has also taught. Schulze has served as a member of the Guild for Organic Environment.

61. *PRISMATIC COLUMN, 1965*
Designed by Paul Schulze
Height: 16 inches

The piece is cut and polished from a single block of crystal. *Prismatic Column* was one of twenty-six experimental designs in the exhibition "Studies in Crystal," held at Steuben's exhibition gallery in New York in October, 1965. Many of these designs were geometric; some were free forms. Steuben has regularly produced such designs ever since, wishing to balance narrative and figurative work with other forms that exploit fully the quality of crystal.

62. *THE MYTH OF ADONIS, 1966*
Glass design by Donald Pollard
Engraving design by Jerry Pfohl
Engraved by Roland Erlacher
Height: 6⅞ inches
Collection of the Brady Hill Company, Birmingham, Michigan

This oval casket of engraved crystal panels is mounted in an ornamental frame of eighteen-karat gold. The glass lid of the casket and the side panels are cut from blown forms.

The casket symbolizes the myth of the youth Adonis, who represented to the early Greeks the seed of life—manifest in a grain of wheat and in the annual rebirth of the earth's vegetation. The eight principal engraved panels show the life, death, and rebirth of Adonis. Eight secondary panels represent the four seasons. The upper panels concern the earth and the heavens; the lower panels, the underworld.

The white-gold frame is ornamented with green-gold leaves. The finial is crystal, emerald-cut. The goldwork is by Cartier, Inc.

The Myth of Adonis is a unique piece.

63.   *THE BUTTERFLY, 1967*
Glass design by George Thompson
Engraving design by Alexander Seidel
Height: 8 inches

Steuben's designer George Thompson conceived of this piece after
looking at tiny Oriental glass beads with butterflies engraved on
them. He wished to show on a crystal prism the single wing of a
butterfly hovering over a vine, the crystal being so cut that, as the
viewer looks at the piece, the second wing of the butterfly is a
reflection, opening or closing according to the angle of view.

  The painter Alexander Seidel, born in Germany, came to the
United States in 1939. From 1943 to 1961, he was staff artist for the
American Museum of Natural History, New York.

  The Butterfly was first engraved by Ladislav Havlik.   149

64. *THE GREAT WHALE, 1969*
Designed by Paul Schulze
Length: 15 inches

This large object is blown of clear crystal. As hot glass, the flukes and fins of the whale are formed on the body. The open mouth is cut into the cold, annealed body.

65. *SEA CHASE, 1969*
Designed by Lloyd Atkins
Height, with base: 10¾ inches
Collection of Mrs. Gratia R. Waters

The piece is in two parts: a narrow fin of glass creates a crescent cluster of five dolphins emerging from a cresting wave. Light from under the separate wave base illuminates the wave and also travels up the fin form to illuminate the dolphins.

Engraved by Peter Schelling, *Sea Chase* was issued in an edition of ten.

67. *CONVOLUTION II, 1969*
Designed by Paul Schulze
Height, with base: 6¾ inches

A crystal sphere with hollow center, *Convolution II* is a blown bubble
cut on the surface so that two wide, flat, interlocking whorls result.
The sphere rests on a reflecting disk of stainless steel.

68. *PYRAMIDON, 1969*
Designed by George Thompson
Height, with stand: 8¼ inches

To produce the sharp luminescence of the base of this piece, a quantity of crystal is cracked into glass chips. After these have been cleaned carefully, they are placed on the marvering table, the metal surface (originally marble—whence "marvering" derives) where glass is usually rolled. There, a hot block of glass is placed on the cold crystal chips, which become imbedded in the base of the block. The points of the chips remain hard and produce the sharp luster of the base. Facets are later cut in the crystal block to reflect the base. *Pyramidon* rests on a wooden stand.

155

69. *ORBITING CRYSTAL, 1970*
Designed by Paul Schulze
Height: 5¾ inches

This piece is a combination of crystal and precious metal. The supporting frame is silver. The crystal and two of the arcs may each be moved into several positions, allowing the facets of the glass to catch and reflect light in many aspects.

70. *MAGELLAN, 1970*
Designed by Lloyd Atkins
Width: 10 inches

This sculptured and engraved prismatic block depicts the entry of Magellan's ship *Trinidad*, in 1520, into the hitherto undiscovered passage to the South Sea now known as the Strait of Magellan.

Magellan, issued in an edition of twenty-five in the "Great Explorers" series, was first engraved by Roland Erlacher.

71. *ONE PLUS ONE EQUALS THREE, 1970*
Designed by George Thompson
Height: 5 inches

A cube of clear crystal is made of two sections cut to form a central
sphere. Quarter-spherical cuttings at the corners are seen reflected
as smaller spheres floating around the center. The piece rests on a
rotatable stand.

72. *IRIS BOWL, 1970*
    Designed by Katherine De Sousa
    Width: 8½ inches

The form exploits the plasticity of hot glass. Here, like a flower, the
rim undulates and is folded back by the glassworker to form a deep,
petal-like contour.

Katherine De Sousa, a graduate of the Rhode Island School of
Design, was a Steuben designer from 1969 to 1971.

159

73. *MUSHROOMS, 1971*
Designed by Peter Yenawine
Heights: 5¼, 7¼, 4¼ inches

These are off-hand, irregular shapes of solid crystal with crimped stems, designed to yield maximum luster and reflection from natural forms.

Peter Yenawine, a graduate of the industrial design program at Syracuse University, joined the Steuben Glass design department in 1969. He has a special interest in silversmithing and has exhibited his designs in silver at the Museum of Contemporary Crafts, New York.

74. *EAGLE DECANTER, 1973*
Designed by Lloyd Atkins
Height: 10½ inches

The decanter is a cylindrical form that has been blocked square, with flat sides and round corners. The flat sides are later ground and polished. The stopper is surmounted by an orb and eagle, fashioned off-hand.

75. *TIERED PRISM, 1972*
Designed by Lloyd Atkins
Height: 14⅞ inches

This tapered, three-sided pillar is cut in three successively smaller tiers. Concave cuts in the edges produce three-dimensional reflections within the crystal.

This unique object was presented to Premier Chou En-lai of the People's Republic of China by President Richard M. Nixon on the occasion of his first visit to that country in 1972. (*Tiered Prism* is represented in the exhibition by a photograph.)

76. *DOUBLE-DISK CANDLESTICKS WITH SILVER CUPS, 1974*
Designed by Peter Yenawine
Height: 11½ inches

These handsome pieces display a tapered shaft rising from a circular base toward a double-disk collar and large bobeche containing a silver candle cup. Four similar candlesticks, with gold cups, were part of the Steuben table garniture presented to Her Royal Highness the Princess Anne on the occasion of her marriage in 1973 by President and Mrs. Richard M. Nixon as the gift of the American people.

77.   *FIRST ANNUAL DUNLOP AWARD, 1973*
Designed by Peter Yenawine
Height, with base: 16½ inches

A crystal form cut from a block of crystal is poised above a column
of stainless steel rising from a base of black leather. Commissioned
for the Professional Athlete of the Year Award, established by the
Dunlop Tire and Rubber Corporation, this design of crystal forms
balanced in tension symbolizes the coordination of strength and
discipline essential to athletic achievement. Jack Nicklaus received
the first award on May 21, 1973.

78. *THE MAPLE LEAF, 1973*
Designed by Donald Pollard
Height: 8¼ inches
Collection of Lord Pilkington

The Maple Leaf is a crystal sculpture, triangular in profile, the front plane of which is cut in the silhouette of the formal Maple Leaf of the Canadian flag. Engraved on the front is an outline of a naturalistic maple leaf. On the back are the arms of Canada.

Engraved by Peter Schelling, *The Maple Leaf* was commissioned by Pilkington Brothers Canada, Ltd. It is a unique piece.

STEUBEN GLASS IN PUBLIC COLLECTIONS
THE HOUGHTON YEARS, 1933-73

Steuben glass of the Houghton years is represented in many museums and other public collections. They include:

IN THE UNITED STATES

Colorado
The Colorado Springs Fine Arts Center

Connecticut
The University of Connecticut, Storrs

District of Columbia
Smithsonian Institution

Florida
Cummer Gallery of Art, Jacksonville

Illinois
Art Institute of Chicago

Indiana
Indianapolis Museum of Art

Iowa
Charles H. MacNider Museum, Mason City

Kansas
Dwight D. Eisenhower Presidential Library, Abilene
Wichita Art Association, Inc.
Wichita Art Museum

Kentucky
J. B. Speed Art Museum, Louisville

Massachusetts
Mead Art Gallery, Amherst College
Museum of Fine Arts, Boston

Michigan

Cranbrook Academy of Art Museum, Bloomfield Hills
Detroit Institute of Arts
Flint Institute of Arts
Grand Rapids Public Museum
Hackley Art Gallery, Muskegon

Missouri

William Rockhill Nelson Gallery of Art, Kansas City
The St. Louis Art Museum
Springfield Art Museum

New Jersey

Newark Museum
The Art Museum, Princeton University

New York

Arnot Art Gallery, Elmira
Cooper-Hewitt Museum of Decorative Arts and Design, Smithsonian Institution, New York City
Corning Museum of Glass
The Metropolitan Museum of Art, New York City

Ohio

Akron Art Institute
Cleveland Museum of Art
The Columbus Gallery of Fine Arts
The Toledo Museum of Art

Oklahoma

Philbrook Art Center, Tulsa

Pennsylvania

Museum of Art, Carnegie Institute, Pittsburgh

South Carolina

Florence Museum

Tennessee

Brooks Memorial Art Gallery, Memphis

Texas

San Antonio Art League
Texas Memorial Museum, Austin

Virginia

Chrysler Museum at Norfolk

Washington
Charles and Emma Frye Art Museum, Seattle

IN OTHER COUNTRIES

Belgium
Musées Royaux d'Art et d'Histoire, Brussels

Canada
Royal Ontario Museum, Toronto

Ceylon
Government College of Fine Arts, Colombo

Republic of China (Taiwan)
National Historical Museum of the Republic of China, Taipei

England
City Art Gallery, Bristol
Royal Society of Arts, London
Victoria and Albert Museum, London

France
Musée des Arts Décoratifs, Palais du Louvre, Paris

India
National Gallery of Modern Art, New Delhi

Iran
Decorative Arts Museum, Teheran

Netherlands
Nationaal Glasmuseum, Leerdam

Pakistan
National Museum of Pakistan, Karachi

Sweden
Millesgården, Stockholm

Thailand
Fine Arts Department of Thailand, Bangkok

U.S.S.R.
Hermitage Museum, Leningrad

INDEX

Numbers of pages on which illustrations appear are in *italic type.*